BREAST CANCER
as a
SACRED LOVE
JOURNEY

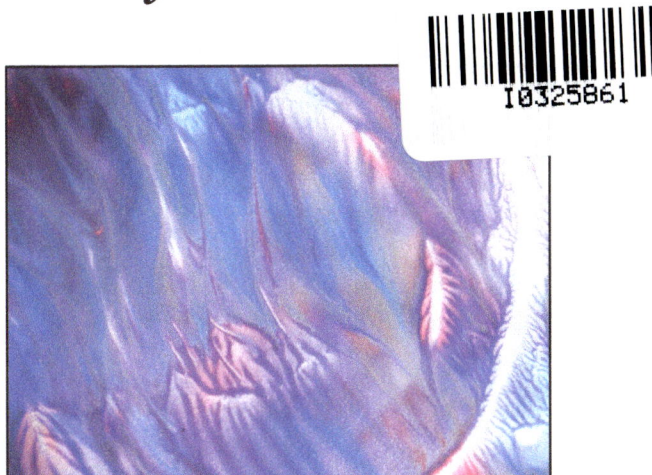

~ JENNIFER ELAM ~

Published by
Way Opens Press
Media, Pennsylvania 2017

Writing and Paintings by Jennifer Elam

Copyright ©2017
Jennifer Elam
All Rights Reserved

ISBN
978-0-9716525-9-0

Published by
WAY OPENS PRESS
72 War Trophy Lane, Media, PA 19063

Email: jenelam@aol.com

Printed in the United States of America

1 3 5 7 9 10 8 6 4 2

First Edition

It's December 3, 2012
and I have just been diagnosed with
triple negative aggressive
breast cancer.
I wonder what that means….

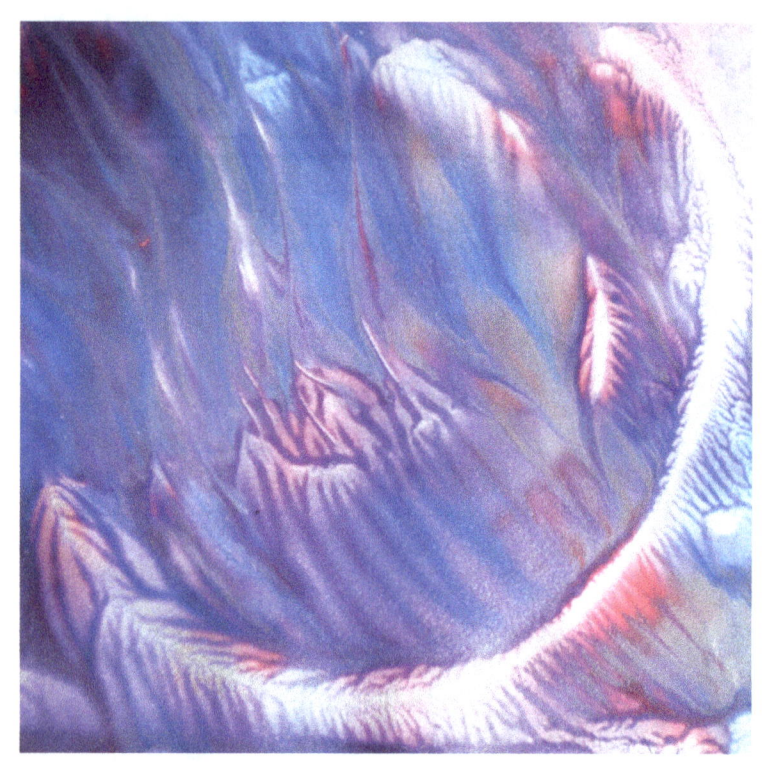

Held in the Uncertainty

Table of Contents

Foreword – In Gratitude to My Love Tsunami in Motion viii
Introduction x

Diagnosis and Surgery: You're Gonna Cut Me WHERE?
Mom's Birthday 2012 1
Nitty Gritty: Fast Dancin' 2
The Verdict Dire: Blissed 3
Jennifer, what are you up to NOW? 5
Reason to Live 6
You May Not Die! 7
Healthy Breasts on My Christmas Tree 7
I Love You a Bushel and a Peck 8
Clear Margins, Clear Lymph Nodes 10
Pink 11

Chemo: But, But I LOVE My Hair
2nd Opinions, 3rd Opinions 11
Clearness Committee 12
I Asked for 9 Million Prayers; It Just Went Up to 900 Million 14
My Body vs. Wise 15
Chemo 15
Chemo Earning Its' Reputation 16
No, Not My Hair 16
My Hair 18
Struggling with My Body's Knowing 20
Bald Woman and the Bald Eagle 20
Keeping Awareness of Life Beyond BC 21
The 500 Year Map 22
The God Who Only Knows 4 Words 27
You'll Do That for ME? Dust My House and…. 23

Religious Society of Cells
Religious Society of Cells 24
Amping Up BJ's (well, everyone's) Prayer Life 25
Fear: Dear Cells, ... 26
Grief Whacked: In-consolable Wreck Today 27

A Joke	29
Hypocritical or Some Kind of Critical	29
Jesus in the Chemo Chair	30
Wait, I Gotta Go P...	30
Wait, I Have to Teach Arts & Spirituality Class: Creativity Saves Me Again	31
From 5 Rhythms	32
Joachim's Heart	32
Karen Died and Now Laura Has BC too	33
Wait, I Have to Go to Oregon	34
Inspired by Moments of Life Lived Fully	36
Wait, NOW I HAVE to Hoop Dance: hoopin' and hopin'	37
Just Like Those De-posed Dictators: Healing Inner and Outer Tyranny	38
Stuck in the Mud and THEN…	38
Cranial Prostheses, Hats, Scarves, and Shawls	40
Susana Gives the 5-year-old Perspective	41
Sleepless Nights	42
Reading from Joanna, the Intuitive – PURE AWE!!	45
Affidity Barrelfuls	47
Met-a-mor-pho-sis	47
Left Right Left Right Left Right Again	48
You Have Friends	51
Wellness Day	51
Chemo Brain: Chalk Dust in My Executive Functioning	53
Easter	54
Artichokes and Flowers	55

Radiation: You're Gonna Zap Me There TOO

5:30 am: Get Up and Drive to Lankenau Hospital THEN Go To Work…Relentless	57
Small Potlucks with Friends: The Bestest of the Guestests	58
Deep Water Dreams	58
The Path of Unknowing	58
Jesus Joins Me on the Path of Unknowing	59
Jesus Joins Me in Radiation Treatment	60
Jesus in Radiation…Still Walking Down the Road of Unknowing	61
Wait, I Gotta P…	61

Will You Just Sing Me a Lullaby? 62
More Healthy Breasts 62
Power Surges…Unstoppable 63
Will to Live and Other Mysteries:
The Grass that Grows Through the Cement (my heroes) 64
The Weeds Are Rising 65
The Bell Finally Rang 66
And BJ Checks In 67

**Post-Treatment: If the Cancer Is Gone,
Then Why Is It Not Over?**
Women's Voices: Living Out Loud 69
But, It's Not Mine: Carrying the Pathology of the Culture 69
Breast Cancer Survivor, NO Thriver:
That Cancer Language Just Doesn't Suit Me 70
Deliriously and Obnoxiously Joyful 71
Finding Meaning; Acknowledging Miracles;
Overwhelming Gratitude 73
Nothing Lasts Forever 73
Pearl-Making: The Gifts in Suffering 73
Art with International Students 74
Well, the Hair IS Coming Back 75
Launched 77
Exercise Class 77
Celebrating Life and Aliveness 79
The Last Piece of the Art Show Finally Came:
Cosmic Images as Possibilities 79
Learnings with Kathy 80
Arts and Spirituality Retreat Days 81
I Track the Path of Miracles 81
Epilogue I 83
Epilogue II 84
Appendix A: Pearl Making 86
Appendix B: Pearls of Wisdom 91
Acknowledgements 96
Resource Notes 102
Other Books by this Author 102
About the Author 103

Foreword
Large Gratitude for my Love Tsunami in Motion

As news of my diagnosis of breast cancer spread, people started calling and emailing me with love notes and questions. Very quickly, I got overwhelmed. I had doctors to visit and lots to do. Not having a clue how one 'does' breast cancer, I sent out a mass email to everyone who wanted to know more and those I thought would want to know...Dear Community of Family and Friends... What came back was knowledge that I am loved beyond anything I could have foreseen. People were kind, compassionate, loving, and practical. They offered to bring me food, go to the doctor with me, go to surgery with me, stay the night with me if I was lonely, play me music, sing to me, send me flowers, clean my house, and so much more. It felt sacred and I felt like I was on a journey of love, of a new kind. A friend from work, Jean, said it sounded like a love tsunami. And the love tsunami stayed in motion for the next eight months, from diagnosis until the last treatment ended and my doctors declared me launched beyond breast cancer. I had no idea this tsunami was out there for me. I encourage you to take a risk and ask people around you to be there for you in your time of need.

As has been said, if you share your concerns and sorrows they divide, and if you share your joys and happiness, they multiply. My journey is truly an example of this.

A THOUGHT FOR TODAY:
It is not so much our friends' help that helps us as the confident knowledge that they will help us.

– Epicurus, philosopher
(c. 341-270 BCE)

Held in the Light

Introduction

Ever since I was diagnosed with breast cancer, I have felt it as very much a spiritual journey. I have felt accompanied by God and the people in my life; there is a powerful spiritual presence in it. And from the beginning, miracles have occurred. The breast cancer just cuts through the layers of the onion of life to what is important…the sacred love journey.

I am very clear that all of our journeys through breast cancer are different. I just want to share mine with those of you who might have heard those dreaded words as a diagnosis or may be accompanying a loved one who has heard the words 'breast cancer' in relationship to themselves. My hopes are that we can feel connected, and maybe there is something that happened for me that might serve as a street lamp in the dark for you. I have felt from the beginning that there is purpose in this seeming senselessness. My friend Jan, who had breast cancer then had bladder cancer, now tracks miracles. I want to be open to miracles.

Recently, my friend Sally said, "I can't wail with you anymore. You handled breast cancer so well that I can't just be a needy mess with you." My heart broke. I am so clear that I did not "handle" breast cancer in good ways or bad ways. Breast cancer came. I was present with it. I went on an adventure with God and a lot of supporters. I was graced beyond measure. This book is written in gratitude for all of that support.

During treatment, my emotions went wild and were interesting to feel and watch. The stories reflect how I went from hopeful and feeling full of energy (piss and vinegar, some call it) to feeling sick and helpless, a roller coaster of feeling. I tended to commit to more than I could do when I was feeling good then had to ask forgiveness when I was sick. I thought, "Oh, the sickness is done. I can do this!" Then, I had to change the plan. Chemo 1 was really hard; then Chemo 2 and 3 went a bit better and Chemo 4 was really hard again. Not fun, but do-able with lots of help and support!

I want nothing in my stories to say to you that there is a right way. Everyone's situation is different and the losses and joys will be different for everyone. I only hope I can be of service to someone out there who is going on this adventure called breast cancer. Guess what! Pain, grieving, wailing, vulnerability, and pure raw neediness are part of the deal that we need to embrace. Then, with grace, there is also enormous joy!! In my experience, they are two sides of the same coin, both to be embraced and lived.

Creativity connects me with my Creator! Creativity is important to me in all parts of my life. Not surprising to me, embracing the creative that wanted to come was a part of the process that saved me. Everyone does that differently too. For me, movement, writing, and visual art are critical for my survival! In my art there are two constantly repeating themes: spirals that I associate with the labyrinth and deep spirituality as well as the spirals that are seen in the stars in outer space, which I associate with possibilities. And second, little growth spurts appear on the paper from playing with my credit card in paint (when I paint, I don't use brushes; my credit card is my favorite painting tool and in my mind is the best use of it). Put together, there is a lot about spiritual growth. I want to share some of that with you so I will share some art and stories that helped me find meaning in this potential darkness.

I invite you to join me.

I intend for the stories to be told in a way that helps you to hear them in my speaking voice.

Spiritual Growth Amidst…

Diagnosis and Surgery: You're Gonna Cut Me WHERE?

Mom's Birthday 2012

When I stopped at the imaging center, I was on my way to get ice cream; chocolate chip with cherries, plain vanilla or both…that was the big decision on my mind……

I had planned a little party for my mom's birthday; she is 85 and doesn't get out much, so I invited people over for a special celebration. I went to town to get some last- minute things like ice cream and balloons. And I had made an appointment to get those extra mammogram images made that had been requested.

I live in Pennsylvania and was in Kentucky where my parents and most of my family live. I grew up as a farmer's daughter. I had undiagnosed allergies and hated the constant breathing issues. I blamed it all on the farm. I committed at a very young age to going to college and NOT being a farmer. I appreciate that life a lot more now. At 87, my dad still farms and I live far away. Such conflict – can't go back and can't stay away. I had been there for about six weeks because Dad had been very sick. He was feeling better and I planned to go home the next day after Mom's birthday.

So, I found the imaging center at Central Baptist Hospital and thought I'd be there about 15 minutes, half-an-hour tops. After being there half-an-hour, they finally called me in for the images. After the images, they said, "Well, now we need to do an ultra-sound" and they had called in a doctor. I said OK and we did the ultra-sound… interesting. After the ultra-sound, they said, "Well, now we need to do a biopsy" and the doctor was starting to get serious. NEEDLES?! I said OK and we did the biopsy. Ouch, that hurt! After the biopsy, the doctor came in looking very serious and says, "OK, who do you want for your surgeon? It looks like you have cancer." SURGEON? CANCER?? NOT ME!!!

My response was, "Hole on jest a dang minute!!! Sorry, but I'm hostin' a birthday party tonight and it's time for me to get back to my shoppin' for it." And in that moment, my southern accent came out, full force.

Three hours had gone by. The nurse said she would call me on Monday with the more exact results of the biopsy. I knew they were wrong. No one in MY family has breast cancer; strokes and heart attacks yes, but not breast cancer. Monday came and you know how that story ended…or should I say began.

By the way, Mom was so happy with the party!

Nitty Gritty: Fast Dancin'

Well, by Monday I was back in PA. First thing on Tuesday morning, I called my gynecologist, who had received all of those reports. He suggested an oncologist I should call immediately. I called and he happened to have a cancellation on Wednesday. I went to the appointment. He was quite nice, met me himself in the waiting room. Before I left, he called a surgeon that he highly recommended, who agreed to see me on Thursday. This was no slow waltz; it was fast swingin' jitter-bug with a fancy tango step or two!

They had been rather dire to this point – triple negative, a very aggressive and fast-growing cancer…serious. In the meantime, I called five of my friends who had recently had breast cancer and asked what was up with this…..Sharon agreed to come with me to see Dr. Bob, the surgeon. It's a good thing she was there to help me process all that information. Dr. Bob agreed with the urgency to have surgery very soon but said it was small and that he "could get it." YAY for Dr. Bob!! So, blood work and an MRI and a bone scan and a few more tests to prepare for surgery.

Fast Dancin'

The Verdict Dire: Blissed

During the time when the doctors were being so grim, my reactions were surprising to my friends and also to me. I did not react with fear, I reacted with bliss. I prayed, "OK God, what kind of adventure are we going on now?" If someone had told me six months before that I was going to have breast cancer in six months, I am sure I would have been very frightened but this blissed- out state was amazing.

I have a long history of yelling at God, so why was I so calm? I remember when I first discovered it was OK to scream at God and God was just fine with it; God could take it (I don't recommend yelling at fellow humans).

About 25 years ago, I was in a deep stew about where my life had gotten to. I was teaching at the university where I had previously been a student. My now colleagues were unable to see me as other than a kid and I was so disappointed at how that was going.

I grew up in churches where yelling at God would have been blasphemy. I had been a very good, obedient girl all my life. Then, one day I started screaming at God and could not stop. In the middle of it, there was a knock on the door. I lived on campus and knew none of my neighbors were home - the plumbers had come to fix a pipe. I opened the door and yelled, "What do you want?" They told me and I said, "Well, enter at your own risk. I am busy screaming at God." They laughed and said, "Give him a few for us."

They fixed the pipe and I went back to screaming. I had about 35 years-worth of pent-up emotions. After about two more hours went by, I stopped yelling. And in that precious silence, I heard, "it's about time you got more real with me." I have always had a good relationship with God, but that day it got exponentially better.

So, why was I so calm?

Blissed

Jennifer, what are you up to NOW?

My housemate, Wayne, is a musician and, with his six bands, provides lots of wonderful music for lots of people, including me. He is a key volunteer for the PA Breast Cancer Coalition Conference. When he found out I had been diagnosed with breast cancer, he suggested I contact the coalition.

So, I went on-line and signed up for their information. They sent me a box full of presents – their "Friends Like Me" care package - books, pamphlets, pink t-shirt, pens, paper, and more. It felt like Christmas –

but the most amazing thing was this. After I signed up, someone called me and said, "Jennifer, what are you up to NOW?" It was Dolores, a friend of Wayne's that I knew but I did not know she worked for the coalition. We talked and she answered many important questions I had. She also said not to worry about any issues related to legalities, insurance, or work because they would have my back on those issues.

Whew!!! A huge load was lifted off my back that I was only vaguely aware was there. And most miraculously of all to me....I had tiptoed out into unfamiliar territory and a familiar voice came back, willing to support me in ways I did not even yet know I needed.

Reason to Live

Audrey came for dinner. That was so totally nice! She brought me salmon and some other food and just fed me well. It was such a sweet evening! We had a discussion about living and dying. I needed to find a reason to live that was powerful enough to overcome this thing that was moving me toward dying. She suggested that maybe just saying to God that I wanted to live, but was fine with living or dying, was all I needed to do for now. And maybe I didn't need a 'because …' as I had thought. I get close to a 'because' when I think about my writings not yet coming to fruition.

And when Audrey started tearing at the thought of losing me, another 'because' came but it was not as potent: because I don't want to hurt others. But that is not a reason to live; a reason to live is because I am called to do work and that it is not finished. My writing fits that bill. And it does not feel right to die when my work is not done; and it is not.

But I was concerned that I couldn't say emphatically that I want to live. It seemed like two pieces needed to be there: I WANT TO LIVE and I AM OK with whatever happens. When I tried to anticipate getting from here to whatever was next (more pain), I got nervous but I was doing very well at trying not to anticipate...amazingly well... that was grace.

After struggling with that one, I got my answer to the blank. God, I WANT to live because my work does not feel done. You know best but I think I could do the next piece of work well. I will give it my best. Please help me resolve this fear related to my work.

A fellow from Bangladesh came to a Friends of Jesus gathering and told a story. His friend was totally committed to climbing Mt. Everest and died two minutes after he reached the top. Talk about purpose being finished! Work being done. Is my work done? Maybe not, completely.

You May Not Die

I am blessed to still have my parents. They are 85 and 87. My dad still works on the family farm that has been in my family since the early 1800s. He has 70 head of cattle that are the center of his life. A family member lives nearby and checks on them often. God Bless Her!

I go there on my breaks from school and provide respite. Telling my family about breast cancer was very difficult, especially telling my parents. My Mom was quiet but my Father's response was "we need you here, YOU MAY NOT DIE!" I liked that response.

Healthy Breasts on My Christmas Tree

Images are important to me so I spent yesterday painting some healthy breasts. Now, they may not look like healthy breasts to you but to me, they are paintings of healthy breasts. I decided that they would make a good topper for my little Christmas tree. But they needed a large feather. So on top of my Christmas tree is now a pair of painted healthy breasts with a long black boa feather coming out. I do amuse myself well! That made me giggle; I hope it has the same effect on you!

Healthy Breasts

(or maybe a butterfly emerging)

I Love You a Bushel and a Peck

Surgery day came and the part I dreaded most was having a wire put in my breast but when that finally happened, it was over before I knew they had even done it. Now I am not going to say that what they did that day was fun because a lot of it was quite painful, but it was do-able. And it was do-able mostly because I was so supported. Shelley came over the night before and did Reiki for 2½ hours. Wow, she really got me ready. Sue picked me up at 6am. I hadn't slept a wink the night before.

Surgery went fine. Since I have asthma, I was worried about my breathing but the doctor assured me that they are great at "airways management." Sue was just amazing. Boy, I picked the right person. She was fabulous – serious, humorous, PATIENT, light-hearted, and just wonderful.

Then as I was lying there right after the dreaded wire procedure, Alice called and sang to me – I love you a bushel and a peck, a bushel and a peck and a hug around the neck....oh so sweet. I felt so loved again....My Love Tsunami continues.

After having ranted about the health system because of the recent nightmare with Pop in the hospital, I have to admit that what I experienced in surgery was competence at its best. The person in the breast center even put her arm around me as I had to undergo those most scary needles and wire in my breast. Dr Hughes and Wendy, Dr. Skarr, anesthesiologist, bless YOU! Then the surgery was over before I knew it; Dr. Bob, bless you.

A Bushel and a Peck

Clear Margins, Clear Lymph Nodes

The pathology report came...clear margins and clear lymph nodes. A new lease on life, so what shall I do with it? I guess I'll start by celebrating Christmas and forgetting about breast cancer for a week or two.

Pink

I was never a pink kind of gal
But now pink is a big part of my life.

Don't know who I am talking about
...breast cancer......
I don't have cancer, it is gone...
So what does that word have to do with ME?

Breast cancer survivor...who is that?
I am a survivor, have survived many things.
Survivor....
No, actually, I am a thriver....

Mr. President, please hear
My biggest dream...o,
I have no idea what it is by now.

Dear God, where is my new life to be?
Dancing and writing and more...that is my life...
How do I get there?

OK, first step, apply for second half of sabbatical!
Oh, Zu is helping me do laundry and Amy is bringing me dinner...
so loved in pink!

Chemo: But I Love My Hair

2nd Opinions, 3rd Opinions

Dr. Bob said he thought a 5-day mammosite radiation treatment would be the best option and then I would be done and the oncologist did not think I needed chemo. So, Christmas came and went and I asked for 9 million prayers from my love tsunami as I faced follow-up treatment. A friend suggested I go see Dr. Marisa Weiss, who is considered the top in her field of radiology. I did.

Dr. Weiss is one of the most knowledgeable people I have ever been in the presence of. She commanded large respect! And she has had breast cancer herself. She said that the 5-day mammosite radiation treatment had not had enough research on it for my kind of aggressive cancer and that I needed the full 6½ weeks of treatment. And she thought the decision about no chemo also needed to be re-visited as my triple negative cancer does not have good options if it returns. OOOOOOOhhh NOOOOOO! She suggested a very knowledgeable oncologist, Dr. Gilman. I met with him and in fact he recommended chemo. I felt they were both giving me the best advice. I wailed! And upped the number of prayers I asked for!!

So Many Opinions

Clearness Committee

Quakers have a wonderful process called clearness committees for when discernment is needed. I have had more clearness committees than anyone I know. I love them. And so, after gathering lots of information, I had a clearness committee. Susan, Christine, and Shelley sat with me and reviewed the decision about chemo and prayed about it. Then we prayed about it more and Shelley gave me reiki. They could envision me healthy by summer; that image was helpful. Shelley and I talked about the will to live; she sees my position of acceptance of whatever happens as healthy. It is not apathy, depression, or giving up anything; it is joining with God to co-create my next adventures. What is this cancer? What is this chemo? What is this radiation?

For more information on clearness committees:
http://www.couragerenewal.org/parker/writings/clearness-committee

Friends Help with Spiritual Discernment

I Asked for 9 Million Prayers;
It Just Went Up to 900 Million

Yup. 900 million. Oh, I don't know how to do chemo and radiation. And my hair? OOOOOO…I need a lot more prayers. I sent an email and said to please send a LOT more prayers. Interestingly, I got back pledges of x amount: I'll send extra on Thursday, I'll send 100 a day, I'll send 22 at lunch on Tuesday… And then a competition started…I'll up your 22 to 52…and on it went. I am quite sure there were 900 million! One community that was praying for me was Pendle Hill (a Quaker center for study and contemplation). One morning, when I went there to worship and ask for prayers, Lloyd, who is a "birthright Quaker" and therefore knows about such things, said, "That is such a modest request, Jennifer. Just compare 900 million to the infinite number that are available. This request clearly falls under the simplicity testimony." He always offers such wisdom so simply!

900 Million Prayers

My Body vs. Wise

Tomorrow is the day. I just took the first pill.
It has started, this unknown and unknowable
Thing called chemo. It is someone else, not me.
But that pill went into MY body. It has started.
This unknown and unknowable Thing called chemo.
I wish I had the faith to do it by faith healing,
But I don't so I guess I'll do chemo; it is
Wise, they all say!

Chemo

The first day of chemo is here (on 1/31/13). Poisons are going into my body. I sure hope they find the cancer cells and not the healthy cells. Drinking all that fluid and getting it through my system was hard. Uncertainty! I have to do the chemo then take meds to mediate the effects of the chemo then take meds to mediate the effects of those meds and finally take meds to mediate the effects of those meds. Claritin, then I can't focus, concentrate, remember, or stop shaking...OK, don't take that again (I knew I was allergic to that stuff). The mediating meds are sometimes worse than the level before.

It was an intense week but my class I am teaching went so well and I went hoop dancin' last night. Those things helped me so much as did my sacred love tsunami of support.

Some things that feel very important: GOD commitment first; Re-evaluation Counseling (RC) sessions with Sue to keep the emotions from overwhelming me; keeping connected with the Joannas, Helenes, Brendas and others in my life who keep in touch with the big spiritual picture; handling the nitty gritty – the house standing and the heat and water on and the bills paid, the family still going, the dancin' to keep me de-stressed and exercised, the social engagements to keep me socialized, the morning routine to keep me balanced, the good food to keep me nourished physically, the right drugs at the right times to get through this period till the time I won't need them – balancing the immediate with the long term with the longer term with the eternal – balance, balance, balance – it is quite a juggling act. Oh, can I do all that?

Chemo Earning Its Reputation

Oh, a virus on top of the chemo… What a week! I worked at trying to stay at work enough this week and am staying home today to deal with my hair. Enough is enough!!! Mucus, no sleep, coughing, laryngitis all week, horrible headaches – from dried eyes, dried mucus, sinus infection, electrolytes, salt shortage, not enough water/too much water (????). Can't talk to the doctor because I can't talk… more mucus, loose mucus, dried mucus, threatening mucus, bad constipation, stomach cramping, hemorrhoids, hard to pee, drink and drink, weird tastes – food is awful but if it's good, it's very good and I want it all – baby carrots, Trader Joe's tomato and red pepper soup…so sensitive to smells, ohhh… Haven't been cold in years; been very cold this week. Now my hair is falling out and my tongue is sore. My whole body is in rebellion! About the time I think it is calming down a bit, new rebellions appear. Night time is the worst.

No, Not My Hair

Ah yes, I wailed! I am not shy about wailing when that is what I need to do. From the time of the decision to do chemo and Dr. Gilman saying, "Yes, your hair will go" until February 8th, haircut day, I wailed inside. This part was hard!!! I had only cut my hair in the 4th grade and when I was 15 and never really short; trimmed but not CUT and definitely never SHAVED.

OOOOOOOOOO, this was hard. Interestingly, some people thought it was vanity and blew off my sadness. But it was not about vanity, it was about my identity. Some people got it… "Jennifer, it is iconic, it is you; I can hardly think about you without the image of you with long hair." My identity felt invaded. My femininity felt threatened. It was deep! And it was hard!

I planned a gathering of friends to help me do the deed. My hair did not wait. It started falling out sooner than predicted. I knew it was going to be a mess if I waited. It would clog my drains and be all over the house so I asked two friends to help me out. They agreed. And too soon, haircut day came.

I have never been less glad to see my two dear dear friends, Sharon and Elizabeth. To do this with me I considered the truest of friendship. Elizabeth is my spiritual nurturer. Sharon cut, Elizabeth prayed and the deed got done! After it was done, I looked in the mirror and wailed. My friends let me wail as I needed to. And because I did not have to stuff any of my feelings, when it was done, it was done. I could move forward. This was one of the hardest days and I will be forever grateful for the holy accompaniment of two dear friends through that day!!

Those are the good friends, the ones who can accompany your wailing. I went to bed thinking that bald eagles are bald, so maybe I could just become more like an eagle and soar…….bald…..eagle…..soar……. see the world more clearly!

Love as a Verb

My Hair

My beautiful hair has always been with me.
I'm told it was black when I was born
Then it turned golden blond. Light brunette
For most of my life.

The bullies called me fat and ugly;
There were days I could blow them off
Cuz I have beautiful brown hair
with golden highlights.

They told me I was too old;
There were days I could blow them off
Cuz I have beautiful brown hair
With golden highlights.

Now, I am told that my beautiful brown hair
Must pay the price for longer life.
It will grow back they say,
And for Samson it did.

Will I, like Samson, be able
To turn to God, and accomplish
My purpose on the earth
As my hair grows back and gives me strength?

Who is my Delilah? Perhaps her name is Culture.
I don't know her name. But maybe,
I will live beyond her influence as Samson did.

Can I please ask forgiveness
before I do wrong? Is it
wrong? I don't know.
I'll ask forgiveness because it might be.

Is it wrong to poison my body,
Knowing it will suffer in some way
And is screaming
that it does not want to?

I feel, I see the screaming
Calming as I ask forgiveness,
Forgiveness for attacking
The body that has served me so well.

The body that has served me so well,
Even when I did not honor it.
As I write, perhaps it IS feeling honored.
Maybe it will forgive me.

Maybe it will get on board,
Forgive me and be not affected.
Reconciliation is possible.

Dear Jennifer,
Now I can cry. I dared not allow the familiar feelings to
well up yesterday, but now when I review the day through
our photos, and out of the "zone," emotions run freely.

You indeed had very beautiful hair; it was like handling
precious art, created of life events, and miracles, and memories.
Love and gratitude,
Sharon

Struggling with My Body's Knowing

Just read the story of Samson and Delilah; he fell in love with her and ended up telling her the secret of his strength – his hair was never to be cut. For money, she betrayed him and he was tied up then his eyes gouged out. But his hair started growing back and he turned to God in a new way and accomplished the task he was put on the earth to do. Can I do that?

I feel like I am betraying myself by buying into this cultural phenomenon of cancer and the profitable treatment for it. Can that betrayal make me weak? And my hair is a symbol – being in the world but not of the world – this is an 'of the world' act – wrong that will cost me – double bind…..is it my purpose to live longer and risk losing the quality of life with this, like what has happened to my friend Karen – is it my calling to have six months of pain and discomfort? Or is it my calling to change my life and live my life so that cancerous cells need not be afraid that their host is going to die? I don't think I know how to do the latter. I struggle with the knowing and the not knowing. Maybe a third option is emerging: do the treatments, not be negatively affected by them, and have the best of both options.

Bald Woman and the Bald Eagle

The bald-headed woman….
I walk past that mirror and that person
is me. Who is that person
that says she is me? I don't know her.
I hope I will like her if she stays.

I am sad because I don't know
where I went. Will I come back?
I hope so. I miss me.

Soar with the bald eagle…soar…

Keeping Awareness of Life Beyond Breast Cancer (BC)

I have been doing some things to keep myself aware of life beyond bc. Friday night after the Thursday chemo, I went hoop dancin'. I did lousy at hoop dancin' but it was perfect for relieving the large stress that was starting to build. I do love my hula hoop!!

I am so grateful for my Wednesday evening times at Pendle Hill in the art studio. I am also very grateful to Wayne, my housemate, for checking in on me morning and night. And his bands that come here to practice, especially Alex with that accordion squeeze box – whew!! I just love that!

One night I was having an especially hard time and they came to practice. I couldn't believe they were there to practice. I was about to be grumpy; then I remembered that this is something I love. So I let go of my bodily ailments for an hour and just danced. By the end of practice, I felt much more ready for living life again – even if the bodily ailments were still there.

Abundant Life Beyond BC

The 500-Year Map

One of My Heroes Has Died...of Cancer. We always wonder why we got cancer and the wondering often goes nowhere. I thought that I got cancer because I am called to dance and I did not dance enough as worship, dancing with God.

But now I learned that my dance hero, Gabrielle Roth, has died of cancer, and she danced as much as any human I have ever known. I did the 5Rhythms sacred dance training with her son, Jonathan Horan, in New York a few years ago.

I read some of what he wrote in his grief. He described how he and Gabrielle sifted through her life and 40 years of doing 5Rhythms work, aiming to build her legacy with a 5Rythms foundation that could sustain her death. They called it her 500-year map.

I decided I wanted a 500-year map. I want to sift through my 40 year career and find the nuggets of gold, the nuggets of god as I know they are there; god being that in me connected to God. Where I did it well....and build on that...for legacy...what will be left of me when I am gone? Thank you Gabrielle for your 500-year map legacy!

The God Who Only Knows Four Words

..."Come dance with Me..."

–Hafiz

You'll Do THAT for ME? Dust My House and….

Adjusting to having a friend coming to my house to clean up my dust took some doing. I have never even had a cleaning lady to clean up my dirt much less a friend. That was humbling!

And humbling is not a bad thing! This cancer has been humbling in many ways and for a person who has spent her life serving others that is a good thing. Some of us grow up hearing the scripture, "It is better to give than to receive" as "It is good to give, it is bad to receive."

So, adjusting is needed. Giving and receiving are necessary in this human life.

And now Cleaning for a Reason is sending me a cleaning lady four times. Winnie is a gem and does fund-raisers for people with cancer.

Just about the time I was having the most difficulty accepting all the wonderful help that was being offered to me, I glanced at my horoscope. Now, I am not usually a horoscope reader but that day it said, "Accept all offers of help with graciousness and gratitude." Whew! God speaks to me in mysterious ways and I felt it important to listen to that one! I had many opportunities over the next several months to learn to accept help with graciousness and gratitude.

Religious Society of Cells

The Religious Society of Cells
By Barbarajene Williams

BJ was diagnosed with Stage 4 metastatic cancer in 1985. She came into her third session of chemo and the nurse was wearing hazmat gear. She looked at herself and realized that she did not have any HAZ MAT gear and SOMETHING was about to come at her that didn't feel great.

After the treatment, she went to a lecture by a physicist and asked what cancer actually is. He told her that cancer cells are cells that have become convinced that their host is about to die and they rebel from the community of cells and start to create their own community. A self-fulfilling prophecy happens and they start to kill the host. So, BJ started talking to her cells. She apologized for the violence that was happening to them in the chemo. She told them they were going to have to cooperate because SHE WANTED TO LIVE!! And she told them that if they decided to cooperate, she would protect them from the violence coming toward them. She lived.

In 2002, a second diagnosis was made in the early stages and BJ took a more radical approach and fed them all gallons of wheat grass and other healthy foods at the Optimum Health Institute for three weeks.

That was years ago and she is alive and able to tell me the story. I heard BJ tell this story when I was a student and she was the spiritual nurturer at Pendle Hill years ago. The story's power but not the details stuck with me then. I called and asked her to tell me the story again now that the details became relevant to my life. I love this story! It is truly the most ultimate Quaker story of non-violent action I have heard.

Community of Cells

Amping Up BJ's (well, everyone's) Prayer Life

Dear Jennifer,

Wail as you must. Throw raw eggs at trees, but ask their permission first to receive your inconsolable state. They will take it, for sure, as they do all the sludge we sling at them in the air. And voila, they transform that sludge into the life-giving green air we breathe. As I remember, you described your cancer as very aggressive. Listen to your doctors; talk to your cells about the hard ride ahead, hard and healing. Protocol for cancer treatment today is light years beyond my two diagnoses. Light years! You will thrive! I am so terribly sorry this is hitting you like a train wreck and, at the same time, I am grateful you have the good sense and wisdom to say so and to express it in a way that can only encourage your religious society of cells. Here's to the amping up my prayer life and your beautiful spirit to listen and follow the way you are prompted to follow. I know you will call for the prayers of all those who care about you; the prayer support is everything, everything. With love and unspeakable empathy, bj

Fears Transformed: Dear Cells,

Surges of power and strength are pouring through me this morning!!! Fears transformed...fears of not having anyone to take care of me if I am sick, fears of going back to work, fears of ...fears transformed that I did not even know had become so powerful in my life...fears transformed into CANCER cells....I need to talk to those cancer cells...

Dear Cells,

I have had all this fear in my body and I did not even know how powerful it was. I promise to embrace strength and Life so that you do not need to fear my death and alienate yourself from the community of cells. That feels like one of the most important promises I've ever made.

Big Love, Jennifer

Our deepest fear is not that we are inadequate. Our deepest fear is that we are powerful beyond measure. It is our light, not our darkness, that frightens us most. We ask ourselves, 'Who am I to be brilliant, gorgeous, talented, and famous?' Actually, who are you not to be? You are a child of God. Your playing small does not serve the world. There is nothing enlightened about shrinking so that people won't feel insecure around you. We were born to make manifest the glory of God that is within us. It's not just in some of us; it's in all of us. And when we let our own light shine, we unconsciously give other people permission to do the same. As we are liberated from our own fear, our presence automatically liberates others. — Marianne Williamson

Grief Whacked:
I'm An In-consolable Wreck Today

A person doesn't go through cancer without some grief and losses. And I call it a whack because when it hits, it feels like I've just been whacked by a 2x4 and usually out of the blue, unexpectedly. Grief feels awful!

About five years ago, I came to a point where I had experienced so many deep losses and was feeling so much grief that I did not feel like my body could hold any more. I went to a Quaker art gathering and my friend, Zan, showed us a 10-yard long painting she was creating. I made a 10-yard long painting devoted to losses and grief. I told that piece of paper it had to hold my grief. And it does. When I have a grief whack and feel inconsolable, I write it down or paint it and put it on that painting that stands proudly in the corner of my room. This painting was not made for public view; it is my personal grief holder. My painting can hold the grief of the world that I take on!

Darkness cannot drive out darkness; only light can do that.

—*Dr. Martin Luther King, Jr.*

Sad and Angry

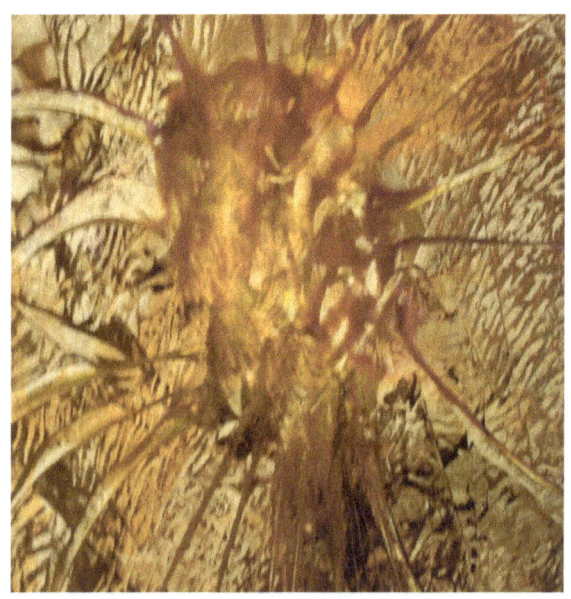

Grief Whacked

A Joke

Here I sit...as the hair falls....I feel like this is a big joke, somebody's big joke – somebody's idea of a joke – I feel duped...my whole life feels like a joke in this moment. My short hair is falling out all over the place. I thought it was cat hair...it is my hair. And my head is becoming bald. I feel lost tonight....just wondering where I am and what I am doing....

My profession that I have committed myself to for all my life, a joke. My body is a joke. It is all a joke. This chemo feels like the biggest joke of all – somebody profits, I guess. I'm being peeled down to the core...somebody's joke. God, are you laughing? I'll probably be laughing with you again...someday.

Hypocritical or Some Kind of Critical

Within a short while of finishing the chemo session, incredible, excruciating pain sets in, not from the chemo but from the exacerbation of my painful bladder disease. So I eat lots of pain killers and soon I am flying high from the many steroids they give me, and I am pain free. That is where I am this morning. Hopeful and ready to take on the world! During the pain, I sleep almost none and learn a lot about myself.

Big lesson: I usually live on my high horse but when in pain, the line gets crossed and I get very righteous then self-righteous and I want people to just be kind to each other and stop the judging, criticizing, and getting their kudos at other people's expense. But in my trying to say that, from a place of pain, it comes out as critical and totally ineffective. Now, that is a good spiritual lesson!

Jesus in the Chemo Chair

My spiritual nurturer, Elizabeth, suggested that Jesus would be sitting in the chair next to me getting his chemo. As a fully human incarnation of God, he cannot escape from those things that affect us humans...like this cancer epidemic...he will need chemo too. She reminded me that I am loved by God as well as so many people!

As I meditated on that image, another image came. I pictured walking into the chemo room and not only was Jesus in the chair next to mine, but there was the Buddha, the Great Chief, Mother Teresa, George Fox, Mohammed, many other religious and other leaders, and all the friends I have and have ever had were all there in that chemo room with me. I was SOOO not alone!

Jesus, I am so glad you are in that chair next to me. It goes a lot better with such good company.

Wait, I Gotta Go P..

The chemo room was a big room with about 20 comfortable chairs where people sit with their IVs next to them. And several had small chairs for a companion to sit in. The room was a very public place.

This cancer is nothing compared to my bladder disease. It used to be that I had some privacy related to my body parts and my health conditions, but no more. Suddenly, the condition of my breasts and my bathroom habits are very public knowledge. That took some adjustment! I used to be very shy and private; well, I had to give that up. My dear friends accompanying me to surgery and chemo are now intimately familiar with my private habits. Thank you, dear friends, for helping me navigate that IV to the bathroom! And to that nurse wanting to change my drugs, I said, "Wait, I gotta go pee!"

Wait, I Have to Teach Arts & Spirituality Class: Creativity Saves Me Again

Before breast cancer, I had committed to teaching the term long class in Arts and Spirituality at Pendle Hill for winter term, 2013 with my friend, Zan. And Oh! was I excited about doing that! So, we did… during chemo. Late afternoon, every Wednesday, I went to class and we did art together. Zan was terrific! The students were terrific! We did string art. We did water colors. We made paper. We made paste papers. We made little books. We made cards. We made medium-sized books. We made big books with Coptic bindings. And we did it all with grace. We went to the fun places. We went to the hard places. We went to the very hard places, all of that with me and all of that with them. We DID Arts and Spirituality well! My student Emily, called it "magic." It was magic!

And at the end of the class, I wrote… On the visionary and very-alive front - My Pendle Hill art class ended this week and we did two receptions: one for the PH community and one for the public. That was an amazing experience that has nourished my heart and soul hugely. The creative/spiritual is always what gets me through the hard stuff! And I had a super dose of the creative/spiritual at PH during winter term. Now I have to find more ways to continue getting the creative that I need.

Human salvation lies in the hands of the creatively mal-adjusted.
  — Martin Luther King, Jr.

From 5Rhythms:

We invite you to stop waiting for a creative moment and realize that you are a creative moment. Remember: it doesn't matter how badly you dance, write, sing, scribble, glue or paint...

Not long after the events of 9/11/2001, a group of us felt that what was missing in the peace movement was creativity. So, my friend Tom and I started what came to be called 2nd Friday sharing, a place where people can share what came to them creatively. Recently, at 2nd Friday sharing, Hank said that he has discovered at a deeper level the value of art. He said art can just cut through the hard feelings like the sun cuts through the mist over a pond. We can express even the deepest and most intense feelings with art and poetry and it is socially acceptable. What a gift!

Joachim's Heart

One of the many Pendle Hill students in Arts class worked all term on a heart. I was so inspired to watch as a broken heart became open. The heart became the forgiving heart then it was a healing heart. And then, wholeness emerged! Recently, Joachim told me that his heart had turned green. His heart is now about healing the earth. Thank you, Joachim, for doing this work out loud and allowing me to see it; you inspired me when I needed that inspiration! Thank you for your heart that blessed me at so many levels!

Broken Heart, Open Heart, Forgiving Heart, Healing Heart, Heart of Wholeness

By Joachim, Pendle Hill student

Karen Died and Now Laura Has BC too

Our friend Karen died of cancer last week. One gift she gave me at the end was the invitation to face the hardest fears I might have in this cancer gig; she was living them, and with grace, right there in front of me. Thank you Karen! And I learned that another friend, Laura, has been diagnosed with breast cancer. It's epidemic, truly!

Wait, I Have to Go to Oregon

During the fall before breast cancer, my dad was really sick with a blocked bowel and he almost died. When he started getting better, he did not want to eat. Food caused him a lot of pain and he had lost about 60 pounds. He had gone from being a very large, strong farmer, baling hay for his cows in the 100-degree heat, to weighing about the same as me. After working very hard for a long time to live, he had lost his motivation.

I asked him if there was anything he REALLY wanted to do while he was on this earth. He thought about it for a few days then said he wanted to go to Oregon to visit my sister and drive down the Oregon coast and into California to see the redwood trees. I bought the tickets right away. Then, when he did not want to eat, I said, "But, Pop, you have to eat so you can get strong and we can go to Oregon." I schemed on my dad and it worked.

We were to go to Oregon during my winter break from work in February. But when that time came, I was doing chemo. I had had my first treatment and assumed I could not go to Oregon. I asked my sister to go in my place but she did not want to go. I told Dr. Gilman my story and he agreed that going to Oregon was very important. He said he would schedule the chemo so that I could go. We went to Oregon; the coast and redwoods were fabulous! Pop's dream came true.

Nature Always Ready to Save Us
Papa by the Redwood Tree

Inspired by Moments of Life Lived Fully

I live a double life. I live in PA but go to my parents' house in KY several times a year. My dad still works the farm that has been in my family since about 1800. I have always been inspired by moments of life being lived fully but since my cancer diagnosis, I have taken notice of those moments even more. I want to share a couple of those moments from life on the farm.

The favorite family cat got killed on the road and everyone was grieving about that, especially the other cat that has never known life without his buddy. I watched him sitting by where my sister buried the cat then he'd walk away then he'd come back, walk around the little burial site. and sit down – poor kitty, he just looked lost. I had helped my sister bury the cat. She sobbed and sobbed as she dug that hole. I thought she was going to dig to China. She loved that cat and kept saying, "Jenny, this is the hard part of loving these animals so much." She has always loved the animals that much.

I witnessed something else very inspiring. One of my dad's cows had her calf by the pond and we drove up just as Dad's helper, Ernesto, located the cow and her calf. Only the calf's head was sticking out of the mud in the pond. Ernesto (I call him St. Ernesto) got in the pond where the calf was, pulled the mud from around the calf and got it out of the pond. He then put it on the lift with the tractor and hauled it back to the barn. All the while the mama cow was fussin' and following the tractor, bawling and was just upset. Ernesto put the calf and the cow in a stall in the barn with straw and that calf did well. Another hour or so out there in the pond and that calf would have been a goner!

I was just so inspired by watching that. That guy put his heart and soul into saving that calf. I told him he was my hero before but now he was really my hero! He just said, "Oh, I got my hands a little muddy."

Watching my sister bury that cat and Ernesto save the calf just spoke to me. Here are two people who put all they have into what they do, work of substance. And they have both put their all into keeping my parents in their own house and keeping the farm going. That speaks to me, inspires me, and I am so very grateful!

Wait, NOW I HAVE to Hoop Dance – 'hoopin' and hopin'

In the summer of 2012, I took six months of sabbatical from work. The workplace stress had been so intense for so long (six or eight years) that I felt like I was coming un-glued. It is often not fun being in education during these political times! My first reaction to sabbatical was to get sick for three weeks. It was amazingly hot and I was spent. One Sunday I was sitting in the silence of a Quaker meeting and just praying for God to show me what to do next. And what I clearly heard was "Hoop dance and rest." I did not trust what I heard and kept questioning. Only later would I know the perfection in the message!

We had gotten through my dad's illness. I was facing chemo – my Arts and Spirituality class was over, my trip to Oregon was done, and I knew that creativity was what would get me through. I had started a bit of hoop dancing the prior summer. I called my hoop dance teacher and told her I needed some extra hoop dancing to get through chemo. It was definitely time! We hoop-danced through chemo and the first weeks of radiation until I could not do it anymore because of soreness!

My journal entry: And today I am ready to go dancin'!!! And I love hoop dancin' – I went to an advanced class two weekends ago and could do nothing they did, I mean nothing. BUT I was so happy to be there with all those great hoop dancers, it did not matter. I have been working hard to keep my life going beyond bc and so far it is working at least some of the time– I again have the greatest sense of this BC as a Sacred Love Journey.

Just Like Those De-posed Dictators: Healing Tyranny Inside and Out

Inside…Trying to build a relationship with my cells was not easy. I tried to be nice to them and talk to them but they reminded me of the violence I was doing to them. I apologized and said I was sorry but that I really wanted to live and this was the best thing I knew to do for them and for me (as if we are not the same person). I felt like a dictator with my own inner Arab Spring.

And out…God did not make me a visionary in order to have me squashed. That is the real task for healing cancer. I have to develop at least a plan for getting life back – life beyond being squashed! You don't have to go to Syria or the Middle East to find plenty of tyranny. In many ways, it is more devastating when it is present but not acknowledged – when the tyranny is there but called something nice.

How to find freedom in the tyranny – that would be the antidote. That is what I need to learn. Learn from a Middle Easterner…that would be the level of irony I need in this. Finding freedom from tyranny is my real cancer treatment.

Stuck in the Mud and THEN…

Today I feel like I am stuck in the mud, up to my neck just like that calf. Minimally vertical…Maybe I am free of the mud but just don't know it yet. I hope I remember to be free soon!

> *"How free do you want to be?"*   —Gabrielle Roth

Free as those gorgeous yellow forsythia out in my yard.

Free as those cancer cells now out of my body to be composted, to transform themselves into something useful and good in the world.

And a short week later...I am really in tune with my visionary self this morning. She said my time is coming.

I've been bubbling over, just joyful and excited about life! Wednesday night the energy started coming back after feeling bad or at least kinda bad for what seemed like a long time. I get excited and giddy to feel that alive creative energy come back into my body!

I chose my healing color for the summer – cantaloupe. I feel good around that color!!!!!

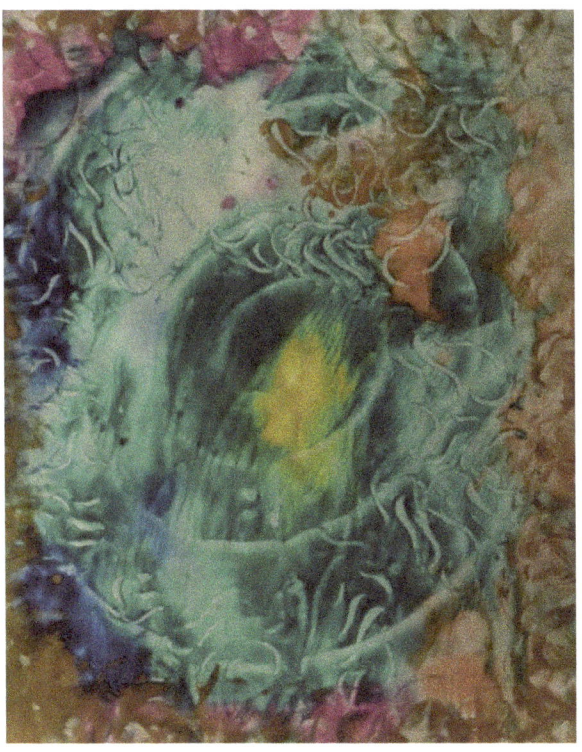

Colors that Heal

Cranial Prostheses, Hats, Scarves, and Shawls

I wanted to get my hair made into a wig. For insurance purposes, they are officially called cranial prostheses (cp). Now THAT made me giggle! I finally found someone to do it for a mere $700; the cheapest one before that was $1600, with no insurance coverage. The hospital gave me a cp aka a wig, as did my friend Sharon. I tried to wear them. I found I did not like wigs and so decided not to spend $700 on a wig I probably would not wear.

But hats I liked! And people started giving me hats and scarves. I got black hats, purple hats, green hats, red hats, stylish hats, floppy hats; a lot of hats! My two favorites were made by a blind lady in Media, who crochets hats and gives them to people with breast cancer. God bless her! But, spring came and those winter hats were too hot. I went to radiation one morning and my new friend Margaret had on the perfect spring hat. She told me to go to Hair Hair to get them. I did and they were on sale for $1.99. I got seven bright colors and had hats to go with every outfit. The bright colors brightened my days. Margaret got done with radiation and had her graduation; she taught me how to do that. Yay!! Her son and her husband were so faithful to come with her every day.

And scarves...lots of gorgeous scarves made by Lynn, Margery, Gloria, and so many more...

And prayer shawls by Whittier Knittiers. Candace brought me a beautiful one from the Prayer Shawl Ministry. So sweet!

And people have been making all kinds of suggestions for things to try when my hair comes back: purple hair, blond hair, eco green hair, o the possibilities...

So Many Hats and Scarves and Shawls

(and that's only a few of them)

But Bald is Best

Susana Gives the 5-year-old Perspective

She had obviously been thinking while I had a meeting with her parents. Susana had been playing nicely by herself during the meeting but when it was over, she came up to me and asked why I was wearing that weird hat. I told her I used to have long hair like her but I had to get it all cut off. She said impudently, "Sounds like breast cancer." I said yes that is what happened, breast cancer. She said she heard there was a medicine that made your hair fall out. I said yes that is what happened. Then she asked if I cut my hair off or did I shave it. I said first I cut it and then I shaved it. Then she said that what she does not understand is why do we cut it off and not just let it fall out. I told her I had long hair and it started making a big mess. It gets on your pillow and in your bath water and you get hair all over and it could even clog my drains. She said that sounds like when the dog sheds. I giggled and said yes that is what it is like. She said she would like to see my hair. So I said if it is OK with your mom, I'd take my hat off. Mom said OK so I did. Then she was satisfied.

Early in the conversation, her mom whispered that someone in their family had had breast cancer. I suggested to her parents that it is good to just answer the questions she asks, no more, no less. Amazing for a five-year-old to remember all that, associate it with my hat, and ask amazing questions! I loved my job that day.

Sleepless Nights

I haven't slept much for decades but sometimes I could not go to sleep at all.

It is 5:46am and I have not been able to sleep yet. The Dexametha has me going….but the night has been productive. I think I can go forward now and live my empowered life, given to me by having breast cancer. Oh my….that is a thought! It is a life-giving, exciting thought! I'm gonna keep those thoughts coming!

Today I gave some friends pinwheels. The pinwheel is to remind us of all that energy that is so freely available. Energy is available to power our engines if we would but stand there and let the Spirit be like the wind and turn our turbines to give us the energy needed to do our work…

Our work in the world... turbines. We need our turbines to provide energy for the callings.

This week I had a moment of 20-20 hindsight about how I coulda shoulda done it better. I was grief whacked. I know I did the best I could at the time. That is forgiveness. Forgive myself and move on to now....embrace the power I have now and that which is coming. It is amazing how many times I have to forgive myself, even more than the 70 times 7 that the scriptures suggest are needed.

Perhaps if you ask me in 25 years, I'll be able to explain the bubbling over I have felt in knowing there is purpose in this breast cancer. Maybe I'll be able to explain how I feel God's accompanying presence with me in this. Maybe I'll be able to explain the love tsunami that has accompanied me on this breast cancer adventure, but right now I just live it and accept it.

Dance with it. Dance with God and others in it! And just do the work—left right left right lrlrlrlrlr..... and do it with large love and gratitude, doing what I can when I can.

"If we set the body in motion the psyche will heal itself."

— Gabrielle Roth

The sun is coming up. Soon it is time to go to work and I have not slept a wink. But what a wonderful night with God! I love the night time!

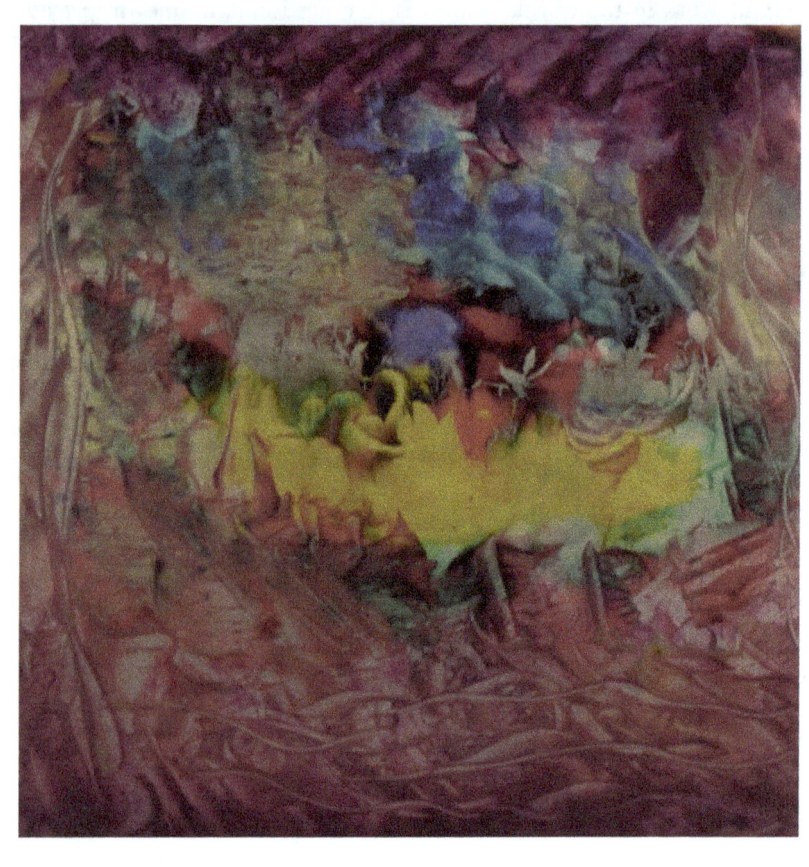

Dancing Through the Night till the Sun Rises

Reading from Joanna the Intuitive – PURE AWE!!

I hadn't seen my friend Joanna in a long time and now she is an Intuitive. She gave me a reading.

Your spirit is saying: "Get me out of here; this life has gone off course." (Your spirit holds knowledge of your life purpose, which is why it is your spirit speaking.) It is focused on something that happened two years ago—a choice affecting life direction.

I get the sense that you thought you were choosing toward spirit/Spirit, but your spirit actually wanted something different: more security, less having to put yourself "out there" with courage. Your spirit is tired; you have carried the banner for paying attention to Spirit for a long time. Your spirit wants to shift into a quieter mode in which you get to sit back and rest, not be a leader or spokesperson. I get a picture of you living in a small house in the country, gardening and maybe writing a book. Lots of quiet time, quiet evenings. Your spirit would like a year of this (and then take stock).

It will be hard to do/choose because it will feel like you are losing everything you have worked for and getting out of touch with some of the professional/spiritual networks you've built up. So it's a tough one for the ego. Sitting in "empty" listening/integrating space, without the usual feedback loops of affirmation for your work.

But really you will be gearing up for even "greater" work. Tuning into where the earth is in her birthing, and what is rising. Listening deeply to the birds, trees, sky, stones. It is a new time. And there is plenty of time. It is okay for you to step out of the thick of it for a while.

It has felt like someone else's cancer because you have gotten fairly cut off from this part of your spirit that is expressing this need. The cancer is a wake-up call that your spirit is not thriving in your current circumstances.

I am now facilitating some reintegration work with your spirit, body, and mind. Dialogue:

Spirit: (Hurt) Why did you leave me there, on the road back there (when you made the choice two years ago)? You just kept on going even though it was not good for me to go in this direction.

Mind: Because people need me.

Spirit: Your first priority is to care for me. I/we have an amazing purpose yet to fulfill. If you want to help people, stick with me, and we will be able to do more than you can imagine.

Mind: That goes against everything I have been told and I believe!

Spirit: Spirit is unfurling a new plan. Things are changing. The old systems of organizing are falling.

Mind: Huh? What do you mean?

Spirit: You need to listen, really deeply listen for the stirrings of change. It is not coming from places of power. They are, however, trying to focus people's attention on them somewhat desperately. The change is rising up, and cannot be stopped. A new landscape of possibility is coming into being.

Mind: How can going away help?

Spirit: Because you have gifts that need to be birthed that you are not even fully aware of yet. You need to bring yourself back into the great harmony (which solitude in nature accomplishes so readily) so that you better understand your role at this time and coming years.

Mind: (looking brighter yet feeling vulnerable) OK, I can try! I will need help. I'm sorry I cut you off.

Now I am re-opening communication energetically between your spirit and body. This was a painful betrayal for your spirit so it will need some love and care. One of the effects of blocked communication has been that you've forgotten how beautiful and great you truly are.

After this work, I get an image of still water and a feeling of great relief. One of your spirit guides wants you to know that after this period of greyness (chemo etc.), there is great beauty and joy ahead on your path. (This angel/spirit is just shining with wonderful light gold energy. Your own inner beauty and strength have drawn such a powerful helper to you.)

Affidity Barrelfuls

My niece, Leah, has always been precocious! She told me when she was seven and trying to grasp the concept of infinity before she could even say it, that she loved me *affidity barrelfuls*.

I am sending *affidity barrelfuls* of love back to my sacred love tsunami today!

Met-a-mor-pho-sis

Spring is coming! Spring is here!! One day I was observing in a preschool, as I spend much of my work life in preschools. The teacher was preparing the most resistant children for a parent program and was trying to teach them a song. Do you ever get songs that just stick in your head? Well, that is what happened that morning. That song stuck in my head for days and I was so grateful to that teacher. The children were not as appreciative of her efforts as I was.

O, Caterpillar, I thought that you were dead;
but met-a-mor-pho-sis
made you a butterfly instead!!

Metamorphosis: Transformation with Fire

Left Right Left Right Left Right again

Doing as much as I can and trying to know when to say enough, asking people to do stuff for me, asking for support and more support, prayin', dancin', fun with folks to balance the hard stuff, creativity!, remembering to say thank you for all of it, large gratitudes, making plans/changing plans/making flexible plans, committing to little that matters beyond work, forgiving myself when I have to change the plans and ask for help, eating as well as I can tolerate, moving as much as I can tolerate and not enough and knowing it and knowing that part will get me in trouble if I don't change it, moving/resting, rlrlrlrl a lot of days, asking for God's help, asking Jesus to be with me, asking lots of people to be with me, asking lots of people to forgive me, mass emails, keeping in touch with lots of people in great detail through mass email, more creativity, class, so many people, so many groups – 2nd Friday sharing, womyn drummers, Pendle Hill, Swarthmore Friends Meeting, journaling, getting a little sunshine, thank you for all of it, daily rituals because I can't remember, keep my notebooks and lists going, pain/pain pills, sit in the warm water, leftrightleftrightleftrightleft...

Left Right Left Right

You Have Friends

I got an email from my friend Maurine. She says:

"Today my friend Will lost a wheel from his car. He stood looking at it in despair and a friend of his happened by. Will said, "What will I do?" Bob said, "You have friends." This story of yours reminds me of that message. You have friends. You are blessed with friends. We are all family to one another. This I know, experimentally. And btw, Jesus loves you too."

It has been such a learning – that there are so many people in my life that are there for me!!! Before breast cancer, I was so afraid of what would happen if something like this happened to me, especially having no biological family nearby. This knowing is such a sacred learning! Thanks, Maurine!

Wellness Day

Ironically, my weakest day in all the cancer treatment fell on Wellness Day. I had committed to going and was determined to do so.

Chemo 4 kicked my butt. Every part of my body got affected... headaches from dehydration or electrolytes messed up, too little salt, or is it my eyes this time? – experiment until I figure it out – just get those headaches to stop, arm is burned from taxotere (and if my arm looks like that, what do my tender innards look like?) and blue from them not being able to find any more veins to put IVs into, burning burning burning, finally relieved a bit from many pain pills, arm pits that smell so bad, breasts that hurt, stomach upset with nausea – though those nausea pills work pretty good... but now I can't take 'em, steroids burning me up with face red as a beat, and more and more... and everything is fuzzy...enough of that for now. I'm going to Wellness Day!

I got there, people welcomed me. I just started crying, got overwhelmed and told them I shouldn't have come because I was too weak to do anything. They got me a wheelchair and gave me a massage and told me all of them had been through this thing. It was just about whatever I needed. That made me feel so much better; then I really cried from being so deeply moved. My friend Sally had called me the night before and asked if I wanted her to come. I told her I thought I'd be OK. She intuited that she should come and there she was. I was so grateful; she pushed me around in the wheelchair and I was able to enjoy so many amazing presentations.

I ended up staying through lunch then coming home. They gave me many amazing gifts — acupuncture sessions, passes for massages, passes for a yoga teacher to come teach me yoga that is good for cancer with a yoga mat, a cook book, and many more things. The most amazing gift was a half-share of a CSA for 23 weeks, with the first box of fresh organic vegies today (translation: CSA is community-supported agriculture and means they gave me organic vegetables that are so good, especially when you have cancer). The love tsunami in motion just goes on and on. And all I could do was cry.

One of Wayne's bands (the one that plays when we clog dance) was downstairs playing music that night and all I could do was cry again. By that time I couldn't clog anymore but I loved the music! I am truly the most blessed woman on the earth.

Chemo Brain

(makes everything feel fuzzy)

Chemo Brain:
Chalk Dust in My Executive Functioning

My friend Karen told me that chemo brain is real! Well, I had been wondering why I couldn't remember things and really my executive functioning (focus, concentration, planning, remembering) seemed a bit off, not horribly but just a bit off, from the usual. I noticed that my balance was a bit off too. My feet have known how to clog for decades but they couldn't move to the music the same way. My feet got confused.

My journal entry: Is there chalk dust in my executive functioning today? Sometimes it feels like there are brick walls in there preventing access to the card catalog. And then I do something like forget a meeting. It feels like there is chalk dust in there just interfering with the memory flow.

I'd say it was the cancer but so many people are saying that is happening to them and are worried about it so I don't know. Maybe another epidemic: Jesus, are you having that difficulty too? God, I hope you don't get dementia....

We forget the important spiritual truths that we have learned so we have to learn them over and over. We need others to help us with our forgetting. Generous...I felt hopeful and not alone in my forgetting.

My cousin Madeline introduced me to a new hero. Here is the link to a powerful lesson in concentration: http://www.flixxy.com/the-incredible-power-of-concentration-miyoko-shida.htm#.UZBuYJV9m-K

Madeline says: My friend forwarded this 4-or so- minute video of a Japanese woman, Miyoko Shida, building a sculpture with the finesse of balance and concentration. It is a beautiful body poem. Thought you might have a few minutes for something so lovely. (It gets even better after the applause.) I found another heroine.

Easter

The day of Pentecost has been intense this year – Spirit fire, energy, and many languages to learn. And now Easter is here!

I just love Easter! It is my favorite holiday! And this year I am even more excited about the possibilities in newness and resurrection than ever! A friend Melanie says it so well. May you be open to exploring the abundance of possibilities in the newness of life and RESURRECTION!

> "...this season I'm more aware
> than usual that these miracles
> don't actually appear out of nowhere.
> The springtime celebration emerges
> from whole circle of the year,
> and the whole cycle of risking
> and living and dying.
> Resurrection is real..."
> —Melanie Wiedener

Artichokes and Flowers

I had four chemo sessions and after each one, my tastes for food changed. And after each one, what I wanted to eat was different. After chemo 1, I wanted raspberry creamsicles. I bought a box and ate them.

After chemo 2, I wanted baby carrots and cheerios with raisins and almond milk. I ate a LOT of baby carrots and had cheerios more than once, every day. My housemate comes up and has a bowl of cereal almost every morning. I would hear the box rattle and get all excited about having cheerios... oh, the sounds of cereal. He said I would probably be sued by Simon and Garfunkel for stealing their phrase (the sounds of silence).

After chemo 3, I wanted pineapple and cottage cheese. I ate many cans of pineapple and actually lost a couple of pounds during that phase. After chemo 4, I wanted artichokes and parsley in all of my food.

My friend Audrey graciously gave me a gift card for Trader Joe's. When I was there buying several cans of artichokes, the cashier was curious and asked me what I was going to do with all of those artichokes. I told her I was doing chemo and when I put artichokes and parsley in my other food, it became edible. Well, don't you know, she went over to the bin of flowers and got a gorgeous bunch, not a $4 bunch but a $10 bunch, and gave them to me and wished me well. I started crying, right there, because I was so moved by that gesture of pure love that came my way that day. Actually, most everything made me cry, but I was especially moved by a stranger's show of love to me that day!

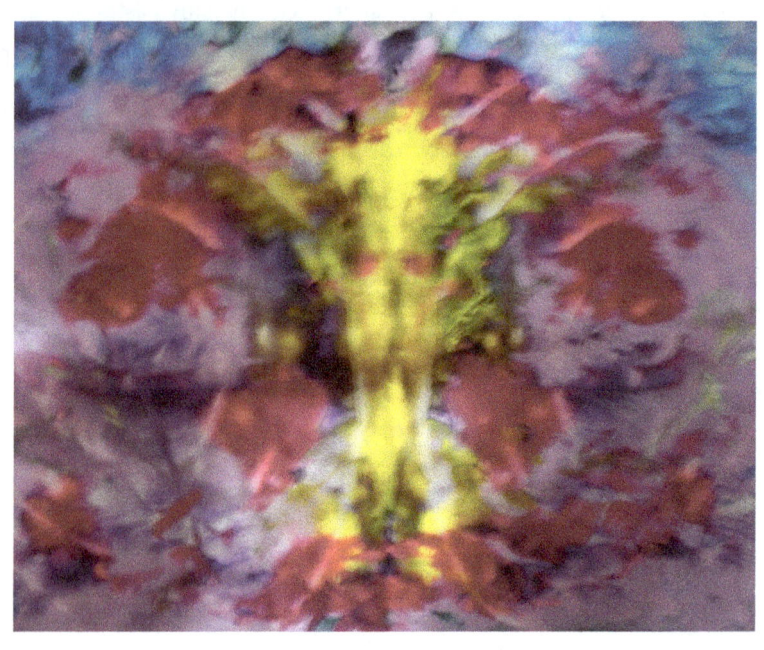

Singing Praises with All of My Being

(even in my chemo blurred state)

Radiation: You're Gonna Zap Me There TOO?

5:30 am: Get Up and Drive to Lankenau Hospital THEN Go To Work…Relentless

The radiation treatments themselves only lasted about 15 minutes but even so, going through it every morning for 6½ weeks when my body was already weakened from chemo was not easy. Again, with much support, it became do-able.

Dr. Weiss is a gem of a doctor. I started chemo shortly after I first met her. She actually called me to see how I was doing. Did you ever have a doctor call you to check in and see how you were doing? I had not so I was impressed again.

At Radiation, there was a special place to park, for which I was very grateful, then you go in and get into your fashionable hospital gown. Then you go into a room where every morning they ask you your name and birthdate (I kept asking them if they had a memory problem), after which you get up on this bed table and go into this machine for the zap. The zap does not last long and it does not hurt but there is this feeling of being invaded, deeply invaded, that was so uncomfortable.

During that time, I just dissociated and went elsewhere. Those dissociation skills come in handy sometimes!!

Today Audrey came to see me at Dr. Weiss' office. She had been there with her mother years ago so she knew that office very well. And she knew the horse that stands there in the waiting room. All over the horse's body is written, "I have breast cancer. I am still beautiful. Look at me."

Small Potlucks with Friends: the BESTest of the GUESTests

Through chemo and radiation, a group of friends came over every couple of weeks for a potluck dinner. They didn't care if my house was a mess; that again engendered humility on my part. They brought food, good healthy food like fresh asparagus, homemade applesauce, roasted red peppers, homemade bread, beautiful beets, baby bok choy, roasted parsnips; and every time it was so good!! They brought good cheer, songs, and just came to hold me up. For a person with a gravelly throat who has no idea how to sing in one key, I do love, love, love music and singing.

AND then there were toasts to health and wellness. I just let all those words sink right down into my poison-covered bones. AND the guests cleaned up the dinner mess! We all rocked!! Just the kind of party I love! And I do love my friends! Nothing like big Love to make us all feel better! O, I am grateful to my potluckers!

Deep Water Dreams

During chemo, I dreamed a lot of being in deep water. One night I woke up after dreaming I was swimming out in the ocean with someone, maybe my sister. I suddenly realized that I had not brought a life jacket or a boat and could not swim. I looked down and saw I had entered the dark blue water instead of the light blue water. I was in trouble! Dreams always amaze me. During chemo, I had many dreams of almost drowning; then I woke up.

The Path of Unknowing

One night I almost drowned in my dream but miraculously got to the shore and dragged myself onto the bank of the river, gasping for breath, grateful that I made it. I lay there a very long time then I pulled myself up, brushed off my clothes, and started walking down the road.

It was a country road, a dirt road, with trees on both sides but nothing else; no buildings, no people, just woods. I was walking down the road, knowing that I had no idea where I was going or what I was doing, but I was happy – whistling, chewing bubble gum and blowing bubbles (don't ask me where I got bubbles and bubble gum in the middle of the woods), and dancing along, kicking up my heels and soaking in the amazing-ness and majestic-ness of the unending beauty of Mother Nature/God.

Jesus Joins Me on the Path of Unknowing

A few days went by and the image came back but was changed. I was walking down the path and Jesus was walking with me. We walked along then we came to a bench and sat down to rest and talk. He was talking to me and listening to me and we were discerning what is next in my life – where I am to be and what I am to do. The answers were not clear but what was very clear was that Jesus was sitting there with me and present with me, engaged in the discernment. Truly holy accompaniment!

Day after day, the image of the path of unknowing returned. As I walked that country path, a dirt road, amidst the trees, I heard the birds, the birds singing their songs, like the morning symphony in my back yard. As I walked down that road, I started to skip, whistle, and blow bubbles with my bubble gum again and again.

A time of change is here…

Jesus comes riding up on his bicycle – those flowing robes on the bike made me giggle (reminds me of the Tibetan monks in their saffron robes on their motorcycles that I loved seeing when I visited Tibet).

"Jesus," I say, "Will you help me discern?"

"Do you mean figure out?" he asks.

"Yes," I said, sheepishly. He seems to like it that I don't usually use big words.

"Discern what?" he asks.

"Discern where I am to be. I keep wondering."

He looks bewildered and says, "Well, I really like being here, walking down this country road. I loved riding my bike here to be with you. And I love being here with you as you skip, sing, and feel the wind."

I did like feeling the wind blowing across my bald head. Loving that response, I ask, "O, may we sit on the bench for a moment? I brought some bubbles. Let's blow bubbles."

"Yes, let's sit and blow bubbles together for a few hours," he says.

Whew…such a relief to know that cancer does not have to be so serious!!!!

Jesus Joins Me in Radiation Treatments

I love walking on that country road…Jesus walks beside me, talking and skipping as the wind blows across my head.

z-z-z-z-z-z-z   O

I jump into the arms of Jesus and am held – tightly – closely – like a baby cuddled. I cling with all my might.

z-z-z-z-z-z-z that sound

It doesn't hurt but invades my body. I feel invaded. Intruded…I am held until the sound stops. O, that machine is finally off.

I can skip again. I can feel the wind. I can whistle and blow bubbles. I can live without that sound …until tomorrow …when I am zapped, burned again…

By radiation.
Remind me.
How does radiation cure cancer when it causes cancer?

Jesus in Radiation...
Still Walking Down the Road of Unknowing

As I continued to do radiation, it was not horrible, not even as bad as the chemo, but it still felt invasive and intrusive to my body. The zaps only lasted a few minutes but as I lay there, I couldn't help but wonder what they are doing to my body so I got a bit anxious. I asked Jesus to just let me lay my head in his lap and sometimes to hold me. Jesus loved that; it was a very comforting image.

During radiation, the image of walking down that road and Jesus coming to join me was a frequent comfort. As always, I asked him to help me discern what was next. He would just say he did not know then notice that we were having a great time just walking down the road together, blowing bubbles, dancing, whistling, singing, and riding bikes...toward my new life.

Wait, I Gotta P....

My friends Ken and Katharine led a week-end workshop at Pendle Hill and I knew it was the right thing to be with them that week-end. From the PH Meeting for Worship, what I heard was that the losses have purpose. This pruning is about getting to the essence. God is there for me no matter what and is always trustworthy. I do trust now.

Katharine says, "Lord, keep me teachable." She spoke about shaping and creating a bowl in which to receive love. Let it fill up and spill over.

George was in the workshop and spoke about Islam having no concept of original sin but a concept of original forgetting. We need to help each other remember. More generous...I like that. I forget so much these days!

Ken spoke about Jeremiah; a cracked cistern doesn't work for holding living water. We apply plaster to hold the cistern together but need the right balance of structure. We get ourselves into trouble when we try to hold onto experience rather than letting go of what is ready to go; I realized I was doing that.

That week-end was magical. I could barely get to class though because so many paintings were coming; "Wait, I gotta paint." I did 14 paintings that week-end.

Will You Just Sing Me a Lullaby?

One night I just felt really bad and I called up some friends and asked if they would sing me a lullaby. My friend Audrey Belle is such a good sport. She sang and sang to me, over the phone. I even have a recording in my voice mail. It was like an angel's voice, it felt so soothing and comforting. My friend Tim said he could not sing to me on the phone but as soon as I felt good enough to have company, he would come and sing to me. And he did. But he lives ten hours away in Ohio, so he had to drive far for that concert; but he did it. He came and sang to me; I was so happy!

Just a Lullaby

More Healthy Breasts

My friend and colleague Alice and I like to bead together. She makes beads, using glass and a torch. One day I went into work and she told me she had a present for me. She had made me a string of beads. I looked at them and asked, "Why did you make me beads that look like fried eggs?" She exclaimed, "Those are NOT fried eggs; those are HEALTHY BREASTS!!"

I showed them to the folks in my chemo unit – even my usually very serious doctor got a great laugh from Alice's beads. (I think there is a large market for these beads).

Power Surges…Unstoppable

Shaky a bit today but getting gradually better all the time. That stubborn feeling is in my head this morning – that grit feeling like I can do anything, just get outta my way – not really a healthy feeling but it has had large survival value for me.

As bad as I felt many days, there were moments when I felt power surges go through my body. I thought I could do anything in those moments and made many commitments that I could not later keep. I am hoping people forgave me. In those moments, I felt unstoppable! I am so grateful for those moments because they gave me hope amidst…hope for doing good work in the world, again, soon.

Morning has broken, like the first morrrrning….black bird has spoken….like the first dawn….

– Hymn sung by Cat Stevens

I had the distinct feeling today that I was going to be unstoppable when my energy comes back. I can't wait to see what adventures I will be up to with God after June, or maybe til then toooo.

Ohhhhhhhhhhhhhhh, I don't want to stay in bed and I don't want to get up. Gotta get some peaceful feelings going. Stirred…lots of dreams….at least I slept quite a bit.

"There is almost a sensual longing for communion with others who have a large vision. The immense fulfillment of the friendship between those engaged in furthering the evolution of consciousness has a quality impossible to describe."   — Pierre Teilhard de Chardin

Will to Live and Other Mysteries: The Grass that Grows Through the Cement (my heroes)

For weeks, every morning as I drove to Lankenau Hospital for radiation, I listened to a CD called "The Will to Live and Other Mysteries." On that CD is a story about the grass that grows through the cement. Grass growing through the cement is usually a bother, so I never really thought about that grass a lot. As I listened to that story over and over, I began to notice the little blades of grass that grow through the cement and started feeling great respect for them. Growing through cement is not easy. That grass has an amazing will to live. I get glimpses of that kind of pure raw energy for life. The grasses that grow through the cement became my heroes.

Grass Grows Through the Cement

And the dandelions that can live through anything…more heroes.

The Weeds Are Rising*

What inspiration I derive
From watching the dandelion
Push from day to day
Until it has
Moved the rock
Split the concrete
Made a place for itself
In a hostile world

What strength of
Character and form
Does dwell in this weed
This disparaged plant
For which
Chemical pesticides
Are purchased
And sprayed

But the dandelion
Lives on
It is strong
It is wise
It is medicine
For those of us
Who see
The beauty of persistence

Brenda Armstrong Macaluso
* line from "Evidence" by Mary Oliver

The Bell Finally Rang

Chris insisted on driving me to my last radiation treatment on June 19, 2013. At Lankenau Hospital in the radiology unit under Dr. Weiss' care, there is a bell in the waiting room. For 6 ½ weeks, every morning, we sat in that room in our fashionable hospital gowns waiting for treatments and commiserating with one another until it was our turn.

On the last day of treatment, each person rings the bell. When I rang the bell, my friend Audrey Belle decided to host a party for me. She brought party hats and flowers and lots of party paraphernalia. I rang the bell and everyone cheered.

In the room, though was my friend Margaret, who had taught me where to buy the best, most colorful and least expensive hats – at Hair Hair. Margaret had rung the bell a few weeks before but then had to come back for more treatments. That was very sad! But she was an excellent sport and congratulated me when I rang the bell.

There was another woman present who I had not seen before, in the back of the room. She was sobbing! I felt so bad. I went over and hugged her and did not know what to say except, "I'm sorry." Through her sobs, she said, "Don't be sorry. You are modeling for me what I will get to do at some point. I want to have a party like you are." I hugged her even harder.

Audrey took Chris, Ruth, Amy, and me out for breakfast to celebrate. What good friends; I love you guys!!!

And BJ Checks In

June 19, 2013

Hi Jennifer,

This is a landmark day for you, perhaps not with the usual exhilaration so much as proud relief and wholistic exhaustion. I think your love and light must have washed over so many during this journey. Of course, it's not over until it's over, like healing, and hair growing back, probably curlier than ever. I know how this day felt for me, like swimming the English Channel thick as mud. Now, it's time to take stock and breathe in the absolutely gorgeous weather showing up just for you.

Congratulations, Jennifer dear. Your religious society of cells did some mighty fine worship.

My love and prayers continue — and don't you forget it!

bj

O bj, it has been a wonderful day. A bunch of people came at 7:30 to watch me ring the bell and my friend Audrey brought party paraphernalia - flowers, balloons, flower necklaces, feather bracelets, and more and the other patients were crying and telling me how awesome this whole scene was and then Audrey treated everyone to breakfast and o my gosh....it WAS awesome!!! And two people came to dinner to celebrate and I got a bunch of phone calls and emails and o my....I was not in mud today!!! I just got back from listening to music in Media.

Tomorrow I am going to Saratoga Springs, NY, to a Jan Phillips' weekend Women's Voices for (a) Change. I think it will be perfect to recharge my batteries. I am psyched!!!

I was wandering around last Saturday saying to myself, "I think this moment holds a million poems." It is amazing how good it feels when the stress lightens up; I didn't even know I was feeling so much till it lightened up...school was out last Friday till 1/6/14 – a half-year sabbatical just started.

Ooooooooo......I am going to develop myself a rehab exercise program to get back my strength. Most people lose weight with cancer but I have gained weight so I have to get that off and just take time to get myself healthy!

My hair is about half an inch long and yesterday, I forgot to put on my hat so I wandered around nearly bald headed and got to liking that pretty well. So I just deliberately didn't wear it today. Got some funny looks (or maybe I imagined that) but it was good!

Post-Treatment: If the Cancer Is Gone, Then Why Is It NOT Over?

Women's Voices: Living Out Loud

The day after radiation was done, I went to Skidmore College with my friend Pam for a Women's Voices for (a) Change conference. At that conference, they talked about Living Out Loud. That phrase has stayed with me. It seems to describe very well how I have lived this breast cancer adventure. Until about age 25, I had what is now called Selective Mutism. Silence is still precious to me. Shyness and large privacy were the norms for most of my life. I seem now to have come full circle; living out loud best describes the next phase of life for me.

But It's Not Mine:
Carrying the Pathology of the Culture

From the moment of diagnosis, I had the feeling that this breast cancer was not mine. Well, it was MY body that went on this adventure so I could make no sense of this feeling (but making no sense of feelings is not so uncommon). While at the Women's Voices conference, I heard a story that made me think there was some sense in that feeling (finding sense in those seemingly irrational feelings is not so uncommon); actually, two explanations came forth.

I heard a story of a woman from the Middle East who wrote a powerful poem about how she experienced what she did because she is a carrier of that pathology in her culture. Are we women who have breast cancer not carrying huge pathology in our culture? The pathology of those who use chemicals and pesticides on our food knowing they are carcinogens, the pathology of those who pollute the air we breathe knowing the negative impact on our bodies, the pathology of ….I could make a list a mile long of the pathologies in our present culture that directly lead to cancer.

A friend also acknowledged one day that this cancer is not the burden of one person; it is the opportunity for everyone to take responsibility for their part in creating this epidemic that certain ones are called to carry the burden for.

My journal entry: But God, I want permission to be not reasonable when circumstances are not reasonable (even Jesus got mad when the tax collectors were in the temple). Our corporate greed (tax collectors) is taking over my temple and they are invited to leave. I have and give permission to not accommodate corporate greed that pollutes our world, spreading carcinogens like they were candy.

Stay bewildered in God, only that. −Rumi

Breast Cancer Survivor, NO Thriver: That Cancer Language Just Doesn't Suit Me

I am not into violence! I don't kill bugs; I put them outside and give them a talking to about staying outside and how much more they are going to love it out there. And I felt like a dictator, with my body going through an inner Arab Spring when doing cancer treatments. I am not comfortable with the language of battling and beating cancer. And I don't want to just be a survivor! I want to thrive!! And so far I am thriving!

And the day came when the risk to remain tight in a bud was more painful than the risk it took to blossom.

−Anais Nin

Deliriously and Obnoxiously Joyful

Blissed out again! School was out June 14th. My cancer treatments ended June 19th. I went to Jan Phillips' Women's Voices for (a) Change conference in New York with my friend Pam and got energized. I spent two weeks caring for my aging parents. And now I feel free to do my life...a lot of people keep asking me how I am. And right now, I tell them that I am deliriously and obnoxiously joyful.

OK, so then they look at me kinda funny and want to know what that means. There does seem to be a shortage of joy around so I try to describe it. My body feels light, not sick. My head feels clear, not the fuzzy that has come to be the norm. My spirit feels clean and clear and wants to dance! I want to connect with people. I feel loving toward everyone. I want to stay away from things that are toxic to me so that I can stay joyful. But what does that mean? Stay tuned....

Last year I was eligible to take a year of sabbatical from work. I thought I could only afford six months and really did not know how I would afford that but knew I could not afford not to take time from work. Then I found out that if you took the second six months within two years, then that was an option. I had made it through the first half so I decided to apply, and trust for finances for the second half.

Dr. Weiss asked me early in treatment if I wanted her to write a letter so that I could take some short-term disability time while doing chemo and radiation. I said no. I wanted to work so that I would not sabotage my sabbatical. That was such a good decision. I could not imagine being off work, sick and sitting around thinking about cancer all the time, alone. I wanted to be off work when I was healthy and could enjoy it. I wanted to be able to write and dance!!!

It was a beautiful day today – my first day off school. I felt so good, like poems were everywhere. I again had that feeling that every moment held a million poems.

And the next day…so nice to take a morning to just be with myself and my openings and a nice bath and be deliriously and obnoxiously joyful again…loving being at home. The sound of the rain is so nice!

Obnoxiously Joyful

Finding Meaning; Acknowledging Miracles; Overwhelming Gratitude

From the beginning, this breast cancer has felt purposeful. I have to acknowledge so many miracles that have happened. For starters, I had no idea I was so loved! I came to live in PA to live in community at PH but learned that that is not a community where one stays for long. That seeking of community had felt like a failure in my life! But I learned that it was not a failure; the community is there, just in a different form than I sought. In fact, it has taken the form of a love tsunami in motion! And I feel overwhelming gratitude. The acknowledgements in this book, rather than the usual page, should take up half the book.

Nothing Lasts Forever

No one lives forever
Keep that in mind, and love
Our life is not the same old burden
Our path is not the same long journey
The flower fades and dies
We must pause to weave perfection into the music
Keep that in mind, and love.

(Ravindranath Tagore, 1861-1941)

Pearl-Making: The Gifts in Suffering

To make a pearl, the oyster has to engage in a lot of friction.

My Friends at the Swarthmore Meeting asked me to lead a forum called Pearl Making, and asked me to talk about what I have learned from having suffered with breast cancer. I had to say first that I do not feel like I have suffered with breast cancer; other things yes, but not breast cancer. I have heard that there is a difference between pain and suffering. I think that might be true. And a major reason I have not suffered is the amazing support I have been given along the way.

The "talk" became a "sharing"; others noted that when there are great losses, it is harder. When a loved one dies from cancer, it is harder. When great financial losses are incurred, it is harder. When there are losses of functioning and way of life, it is harder. When chronic pain is involved, it can wear a person down. When the losses are permanent, it is harder. I experienced none of these with the breast cancer. I am grateful!

The sharing was intimate and beautiful - sweet sweet morning. In response to a query about how to make suffering redemptive, Friends shared a lot of wisdom and I felt enormously blessed. (See Appendix A).

Art with International Students

My friend, Rebecca asked me to do art, making hand-made journals with 20 international students through the Dialog Institute and funded by the State Department. They were all from Egypt, Iraq, Turkey, and Lebanon. They gave me perspective.

THEY experienced the external Arab Spring! They had done a project earlier in the week in which they made huge posters. They put their own pictures at the top then a picture of the person in the world that had inspired them most, then a picture that represented who they wanted to inspire. They wrote about each of those things. I cried as I read them; I was so moved by their commitment to peace and recognizing the challenges they face on that path (not that I can even know).

They came to the studio and as they made their journals, they all laughed and had so much fun! They spoke Arabic most of the time. When I had them come back to the circle and talk about what they had been doing, they had been talking about their different countries and learning from each other about different aspects of civil war and peace work. It was truly amazing! They told me this had been a huge icebreaker. They had not had a chance to just be creative together, laugh and have fun, and they loved it. I was so pleased.

This is the most hope I have felt about the Middle-East situation and the world situation really in a very long time. I think I'll quit watching the news and just interact with people in these countries and commit to arts and activism. I was truly impressed. I want to work for the Dialog Institute when I grow up, or retire, or some such. I was so blessed to hear them talking to one another with such hope for the future for their countries. I am so grateful for the inspiration of youth when situations seem so hopeless. I am inspired....life beyond breast cancer truly exists.

Early on, I had felt like I had been involved in an inner civil war with an inner Arab Spring. I felt especially blessed to meet young people who had done the external version of the Arab Spring and were finding their way to peace.

Well, the Hair IS Coming Back

When I was grieving the loss of my hair, I can't tell you how many people said, "O honey, it'll come back." Although my brain knew they were right, at that moment the rest of me wanted to just hit somebody when they said that. So WHAT? I wanted to say. I need to grieve the LOSS of it NOW.

Well, my hair is coming back, full force. It seems to be a little confused. It is coming back full force ON MY FACE. Now, what do I do with a beard? I went on-line (where we go to get answers these days) and it seems that this happens to lots of people and there was some encouragement that, left alone, the beard would likely sort itself out.

And what am I supposed to do with SHORT HAIR on my head? I have never HAD short hair. And it is gray, not brown. I look in the mirror and wonder who this person is.

And then...I woke up one morning and my hair was curly. I've never had short hair, gray hair, or curly hair. O, the confusion goes on and on.

My friends with short gray hair offer great advice for hair dressers. HAIR DRESSERS? I have never had a hair dresser. How does one relate to HAIR DRESSERS? And I suppose they want real MONEY to dress my hair! O, not only is my hair confused but I am totally baffled at these new arrangements.

Now, some friends have suggested this as an opportunity to play…well, I am almost always up for that. They say to try different things – OK, we'll see what appears NEXT on my head. Maybe bald wasn't so bad…I met a woman at a wedding a few months ago that has been bald for 20 years. She was gorgeous. I told her she was my new heroine…boy, how life and perspective can change in a few months…stay tuned……

Some days I still can't take in all that has happened in the last months and I say to friends: "You wouldn't believe this because I can't believe it yet…one day I will sit with the wind blowing through my very short

Coming Back But a Little Fuzzy and Confused

Launched

I lead a double life (maybe triple and quadruple); I live in PA but go back to where I am from in KY several times a year. I started my Quaker life in Berea, KY but recently, I have not had transportation available to get to Berea on Sunday morning so I started attending the Lexington Friends Meeting more frequently. Since I have had breast cancer, Lexington Friends have sent me untold numbers of cards, letters, and emails supporting me.

Recently, when I was in KY, my friend Betty had a potluck dinner in my honor and Friends came. She called it my launching party…launched past breast cancer. I then went to my follow-up visits to see Dr. Weiss and Dr. Bob. I told them that I needed clearance for launching. They gave clearance. I am launched into post BC!!

Exercise Class

Say it again: *"If we set the body in motion, the psyche will heal itself"*
— Gabrielle Roth

I am trying to get my strength back by riding my bike, dancing, hooping, going to exercise class at Riddle Hospital's program, and just trying to move more. Never enough exercise! Once I get into the moving, I love it; but getting started is just so hard.

The first day at exercise class, there was my friend Jacquie. I hadn't seen her in forever. We got excited and disrupted everyone's solemn exercise routines with our hugs and laughter. Strengthening is slow but boot camp with Katy (the teacher) will get me there! And I am still enjoying my CSA vegetables that will help to make me strong – yay for Unite for Her!!

Launched

Celebrating Life and Aliveness

I tried to have a birthday celebration last year but it never worked out. I invited about a hundred people to my house then left when my dad got sick. Fortunately, most of them got the word not to come.

But, this year it happened! I invited everyone I thought would want to celebrate LIFE and ALIVENESS with me. And we did celebrate! There was so much music, thank you Wayne! There was cloggin' and swing dancin'! There was drummin' and singin'! There were people there just loving me and loving each other well. Kindness in abundance! A sacred love journey continuing....

I laughed so hard that my water broke and I wasn't even pregnant.
– Author unknown

The Last Piece of the Art Show Finally Came: Cosmic Images as Possibilities

All through chemo and radiation, I had to do art; I had to paint. Creativity saved me. And it seemed like the paintings were almost complete, the show was almost done. But, there was a bit more…I have never had a baby but it felt like I was having labor pains. It was there, it was so close, but it would not come. I needed to look at cosmic images. In the cosmic images, I saw many spirals, like I see in my art. I saw color and texture, like in my art. What was it in those cosmic images that drew me to them, compulsively? I kept looking at them, for weeks. Then it came, MY cosmic images, not so different from my usual art. The spirals are there, along with colors and texture. But brilliant and rich and deep colors…representing POSSIBILITIES!!!

I can't wait to share this art with everyone!

Cosmic Possibilities

Learnings with Kathy

Yesterday Kathy called. She was desperately depressed and in the dark. I listened for over an hour. Her theme was self-loathing and self-sabotage. She had sabotaged her job, her living situation, and her relationship. Oooohhh…she said that my friend Betty had told her I had breast cancer and was cheerful about it; how did I do that? How did I get beyond the self-loathing, self-sabotage and desperation? How do I know that the dark places are purposeful? I have known self-loathing in the past, but not now. What is different? I need to articulate the beginning thoughts that came in response to Kathy's questions.

See Appendix B for Pearls of Wisdom that came related to Kathy's questions.

Arts and Spirituality Retreat Days

Frank said that he has been fighting depression for months. He has discovered at a deeper level the value of art. Art can just cut through these hard feelings. We can express it all no matter how intense it gets in acceptable ways with poetry and art. So, I keep facilitating arts and spirituality retreats.

I was so moved recently when friend Jan, who had breast cancer and then bladder cancer, discovered a true calling: tracking miracles. She wrote:

I Track the Path of Miracles

After years of healing the memories of earlier times
In a long distance race that seemed like it would never end,
I am nearing the finish, only to discover that
Spirit was there all along
Just needing to be revealed.
The pain needed to be peeled off, layer by layer,
Like an onion until it is ready to join with
The nourishing fragrance of the soup, or the stew.
Tears flowed endlessly, as the layers were peeled away.
It was a work unfolding, leading to a savory feast.
A feast of healing.
And now,
Now, I am now tracking the path of miracles.

I am tracking the path of miracles.
Like a condor, perched on the cliff's edge
Waiting to step off,
To join the thermals that will carry it aloft.
Gliding with its nine-foot wing span
Where it will travel miles and miles, effortlessly.

I too track the path of miracles
While waiting on the edge of the cliff
Ready to step out and
Join the currents that will hold me aloft.
Learning to trust, learning to let go of fear,
As I track the path of miracles.
  — Jan Alexander

Friend Lisa, who has also had breast cancer, kept reading Jan's words over and over, taking them in. Doing art and writing poems connects us to one another at a deep level. Doing art connects me to my Creator; my Soul made visible as a link to the Infinite – that of God in me connected to the Bigger.

Epilogue I:
So, What's Next, Jennifer?

Love is a fruit in season at all times, and within reach of every hand.
  – Mother Teresa

Where there is great love, there are always miracles.

  – Willa Cather

Well, it is October and soon I go for my next mammogram; it's been a year since my last one. What's up for the future? I don't know. My dear dear friend just learned that her breast cancer is back. Another dear one got bladder cancer after breast cancer; she tracks miracles now. And another friend had it come back three times. Another has been disabled. Another died. And those things are scary!

And there are a bunch of friends who had breast cancer and it never came back! YAY! I will do my best to be one of them.

A fish cannot drown in water,
A bird does not fall in air.
In the fire of its making,
Gold doesn't vanish; the fire brightens.
Each creature God made must live
Its own true nature;
How could I resist my nature,
That lives for oneness with God?

  – Mechtild of Magdenburg

I hope to find my truest callings and live into them!

My horoscope said:

You're ready to expand your horizons...Just break out of the cage that has been imposed on you.

Are you in a place where your best strengths can be used? What good would a sundial do in the shade? —Author unknown

Friend John Calvi recently gave a talk at Pendle Hill. What I remember most is: in order not to burn out when doing ministry, one has to be living the life they really want to live.

I will walk the rocky mountain sowing...
my life as the grass growing through the cement,
responding to those who ask me for help,
listening to and accompanying intense emotion, and
following my truest callings as best as I can figure out how...

But, whatever happens, I am so grateful for the knowledge of God's presence in my life and for the support of all those people in my life that are available and show up to live life so fully each moment that we have. Thank you for sharing this bit of life with me!!

Epilogue II

Well, it is now four months after finishing all cancer treatments. I am in horrible pain and the doctors say it is nerve pain related to damage done by the cancer treatment. Ohhh....I thought I had gotten through the cancer and was so relieved. Well, I AM through the cancer, but what is this? Now what do I need to do?

Life's Passion Cannot be Hidden

Appendix A

Pearl Making: Finding the Gifts in Suffering

Sharings from a Forum at Swarthmore Friends Meeting

- We never know the impact of an event so it is good to hold it all lightly; holding our experiences lightly is very different from denying them or denying our feelings in the experiences. This wisdom story was shared: The farmer's oxen died and he went up the mountain to the wise man and told him the oxen had died and it was terrible; the wise man said "Maybe so, maybe not." Then a herd of wild horses came by the farm and the farmer got a horse to do his farm work and told the wise man of his good fortune; the wise man said, "Maybe so, maybe not." In trying to tame the wild horse, the farmer's son broke his leg and the farmer told the wise man of his misfortune and the wise man said, "Maybe so, maybe not." Then the army recruiters came to draft the son for war, but couldn't because his leg was broken so the farmer told the wise man how great it was that his son was not drafted for war. And the wise man said...and so the story goes on and on. I have felt like this farmer in my breast cancer. Misfortune turning to blessing...honoring grief and loss and feeling what I feel then moving on to the blessings.

- Whether or not an experience becomes a suffering has a lot to do with whether the experience is accompanied with fear or love. When fear is present, one needs to feel it and allow the energy of it to move toward love. We need to feel all of our feelings that come, hold them lightly, and let them go when they have served their purpose. In our culture, we get the message all around us that grief is not OK; experiencing our grief is important so that we can experience our joy just as deeply.

- Acknowledging how blessed we are, privileged really, because so many come from backgrounds of not sharing with others when life gets difficult. Sharing in intimate ways is such a special blessing!

- Holy accompaniment is a concept I learned years ago from the peace teams that travel to war zones and accompany the people; just the fact that the peace teams are there often keeps the threatened population safe. Holy accompaniment by God and each other is so important!

- Feeling our feelings as we feel them, expressing them authentically, then moving on with a clean slate is important. Be true to yourself and your own experience!

- For some, hearing from others who have had cancer was often just as helpful and sometimes more helpful than advice from professionals.

- A Friend talked about acceptance — Jesus said "Suffer the little children to come to me," by which he meant "accept" the children. When we are vulnerable, we become like children. Difficulties can be opportunities to be led by the Light.

- Another Friend noted that acceptance of what is can lead to pain not being suffering. A friend said, "Just because I'm in pain doesn't mean I have to suffer." Suffering = Pain x Resistance.

- Quote from Isaiah (paraphrased): "The Lord may send you troubles, but your Teacher will not hide from you." Hearing these things helped during a hard time. Note that acceptance does not mean acceptance of injustice, wrongness, or people hurting one another without action.

- A friend noted that sometimes she does not want to burden others with her difficulties and ends up being alone in it. But others pointed out that Friends are often honored to be asked to accompany Friends in their time of difficulty. Holding one another is a privilege. Another Friend queried, 'The love surrounding Jen protected her; so many people suffer due to isolation, even though surrounded by plenty. How can we help people with that?"

- Building a context for experience is important. Experiences occur for our spiritual growth and learning. With that context, the experience becomes something very different than when we see it as just something horrible that happened to us.

- Optimism has its place but the timing is important. Be sensitive to where the person is on the journey and what they need then. For example, losing my hair was very hard. Before I had it cut, I was very sad about what was going to happen. People kept saying "O, it will grow back." Well, obviously that statement is true. And is a fact that I knew in my head. When I was in grief, however, that was not a helpful statement. It was not yet time to fix the problem. It was time to be empathetic. I needed to hear, "I am sorry you are losing your hair." The redemptive message and timing are critical for it to be heard – at the wrong time it seems superficial.

- A Friend shared lessons from a stroke she suffered in her early 30s at the same time her marriage was failing. Eventually it was possible to see it as a "stroke of good luck." Challenges were conquered. She no longer sees herself as a victim and no longer blames others for the stress leading to a stroke.

- A Friend offered: When I have suffered, I was immersed in it, stuck, and experienced large losses; it was, relentless!

- Another Friend offered: I recently traveled to Bhutan, and I could feel the influence of Buddhism. People are peaceful, compassionate, accepting (despite very difficult living situations). Buddhism has much in common with Quakerism.

- Just as the fish doesn't know what water is, we don't know what air is, until we're without it. Similarly, we can take for granted a pain-free life until the pain knocks on our door.

- Chronic pain can last through generations. For example, one family had an abusive grandfather, and people in the family are still tight, "mean," even years later. Once you recognize that's not who you are, trust opens up.

- Suffering is the human condition. Pain can be a touchstone for change and help to get the parts of life into balance.

- Jen's cancer is our cancer as a community, part of our fabric; we want to let her know "we want to be part of it with you." Sometimes people say unfortunate things to a person with cancer because they're scared.

- "What doesn't kill you makes you stronger" – that old saying may be true related to emotional & spiritual strength. Look at the resilience of trees…the sharper the winds the tougher the timber.

- It can be devastating to think of all the people we know with cancer, but the point is that they not face it alone. We're so blessed to have this group, our meeting, to talk to. It's an honor to be able to support someone with cancer, to see through this adversity how much we treasure them.

- Jen was an example to us about losing her hair. She didn't say "It's nothing." She noticed and made a ceremony of it. Children getting to touch her cut-off braid; that was meaningful to them.

- It helps to see someone "enveloped in a white cloud of love."

- Timing is important. Sometimes we need to grieve, which is not a negative thing but an important part of our work.

- It's important to hold things lightly. Don't take a cancer diagnosis too seriously; it's an adventure "God, what's next?" That's different from denying. (Chronic pain is hard to do that with, though.)

- A family that is all about shame is devastating; it creates isolation and fear. Family dynamics can prevent accompaniment.

- Men are especially burdened by shame—not feeling it's OK to share their pain. How can we lift that burden?

An example was given of an undemonstrative father who became much more generous & open through caring for his wife through a degenerative disease. He wrote, "If there's a God (and especially if there's not), I'm doing his work." His kindness was hidden before all this and it showed up first in the guise of duty.

Jennifer shared about how much she now values authenticity, even more than before. The gifts and lessons have been huge. Her experience led her to learn many things more deeply, to peel away the layers of the onion.

We began and ended with silence.

And Body Prayer: Praise You (reaching upward); Bless me (arms folded across the chest); To do Your work in the world (arms extend out with palms up and hands extended); Thank You (hands folded in prayer position). Then we formed a circle, drawing love in and extending it out to each other and the world with our hands.

The huge spiritual lessons have related to: the non-duality of strength and vulnerability, the importance of gratitude, and the goodness in the human heart that we don't hear so much about – all continue in the forefront. And most of all, we are accompanied by God and each other, so we are never alone, no matter how lonely we might feel.

Appendix B

Pearls of Wisdom *(in response to Kathy)*

- God/faith/grace – God don't make junk – God has purpose for ALL.

- Tell the truth as I know it!

- Friends are those who hold me in my strength when I can't; find those who can.

- Honor all emotions that come, no matter how intense. Honoring intense emotions tends to prevent acting out. I have learned not to be afraid of them, when I honor and paint them.

- Be very careful what words I use; be careful of ALL that I allow into my psyche.

- Do NOT watch violence on TV or movies.

- Constant self-examination, honestly, compassionately.

- Do NOT allow judgment by self or others; put my judge on the shelf at times; need it if I am going to cross a street but not for deciding my worth.

- EMBRACE creativity, whether it is painting, piano, lesson plans, psych evals, whatever…do it creatively.

- Allow what comes nonjudgmentally; hold it all lightly as "stuff," not as who I am.

- Accompaniment is very important, as are containers for holding all that is.

- Eat healthy, exercise, take care of your body!!! Find passions: Yoga, qigong, etc.

- Find someone to check in with daily until you can make some small steps forward and get back into community and safety net.

- It is blessed to RECEIVE as well as GIVE – balancing act! Some of us grew up with the scripture that says, "It is more blessed to give than to receive" as meaning "It is good to give, bad to receive." It is also good to receive. We are to love our neighbors as ourselves. That says we need to love ourselves too. For some, that is hard.

- Find symbols to connect to: find and replace symbols in your life that don't work; for me bald eagles were really important to relate to.

- When I want to be inspired, I go online and watch Mama Gena sing Firework. I listened to a CD called, "Will to Live and Other Mysteries." These inspirations are important; listen over and over as needed.

- DANCE wildly and generate endorphins!

- Fall in love with yourself! Focus on what is so right about yourself until you do!

- PRAY, talk to God, listen...

- Be good to MY FRIEND – YOU

- ASK for what you need from those around you, a little at a time from each, but you can't ask for what they don't have to give.

- Find words of wisdom that speak to you and post them all around you.

- Find mantras that work for you and say them over and over.

- Develop spiritual disciplines to prevent the desperation coming again. For me, a review of the day asking where was God working for me today and what might I need to do differently, works wonders.

- Find your deepest self below the noise and trust her! Sit in silence every day and listen! Enjoy nature!

- Write a poem from your truth – self-loathing may be the title.

- Watch the sun come up and embrace the new day, letting go of the hard stuff until it is time to deal with it, a small piece at a time.

- If doing therapy, contract to end on an inspirational note.

- You don't have to confront everything all at once – quote mentor Dorothy Tredennick.

- Accept life is not always easy, not even often easy; commit to enjoying everything, no matter what comes. When you are not enjoying something, don't lie. Accept when you don't and go about committing to the enjoyment again – many times a day.

- Forgive yourself and others a million times a day – that is not the same as saying abuse is OK. Look for opportunities to experience love in a million ways and receive it in a million ways.

- Ask for 90 million prayers and more when needed.

- Journal journal journal – or whatever it takes to get it out of you.

- If you are still breathing and your heart is still beating, there is a spark of life force somewhere in there. Find that spark and tend it till the fire starts blazing again! Find the spark of your truest and highest SELF trying so desperately to come through; that is a big part of what depression is, that spark trying so desperately to be tended.

- Start somewhere; small starts are fine. What CAN you do? For you? For someone else in need but not to avoid your own needs? You and they count.

- Embrace the faith of the birds and lilies of the field.

- How can you connect with others? In small ways? In healthy ways? You are being called to deeper and healthier…purpose in all, just KNOW that.

- Be careful who you talk to about what; talk to those who will not fear you; you have enough fear, you don't need theirs too. Even therapists are prone to fear. You don't need their fear!

- You are in this world for a purpose. Find something outside yourself to commit to that makes you feel purposeful…at the first hint that your own health is not going to take every ounce of your energy.

- If you need to stay in bed all day, stay in bed all day; just don't beat yourself up for it. When you possibly can take a baby step, take a baby step and as soon as you can take a bigger step, take a bigger step.

- Left Right LRLR is the best we can do at times. Do it!

- KNOW there is joy out there to be had. Find it. Receive it. Begin with a drop and build. What brings you the tiniest joy? Embrace it.

- Have a spiritual nurturer who knows how to pray for you!

- Connect with others; let them know what is happening in ways they can handle.

- In helping to find a reason to live and making your life count: prioritize children; create integrity, commitment, and faithfulness in your relationships rather than just usefulness; love God and your neighbor, and everyone is your neighbor – love as a verb, build communities in your life – love and enjoy them; get help discerning your gifts and callings and know your contributions can make a big difference in changing the world; know what is enough; discern and live your values, modeling them; make ethical practice in your business a priority. Do well by doing good, find what breaks your heart most in the world and work to transform that – do work of substance, study the policies, morals and politics of your politicians and hold them accountable, know what you stand for, know what you would give your life for and you will know what you can live your life for.

Acknowledgements

Gratitudes (the risk in doing this list is that undoubtedly I will miss someone; please forgive me if that is you – there has been a love tsunami that comes my way and I can't always keep up with the thank yous so I ask forgiveness in advance if you are not on the list – does not mean I don't love and appreciate you – just blame the chemo brain that I have learned is real);

To those friends who did breast cancer before me and taught me what to do first, second, third and next: Amy Rubenstein, Sharon Gunther, Helene Pollock, Lisa Sutton, Joan Broadfield, Barbarajene Williams, Jan Alexander and Melissa – and the many new friends with breast cancer that I made along the way on this love journey;

All those with other cancers who gave me lessons, especially Karen, Nancy, and Alice;

To my parents, David and Margaret, and family who prayed for me;

Mary and Paula – sisters taking care of parents while I am away for the longest time ever – what angels they are! Ruth and Rachel – who help take care of my parents – so grateful for them!!! And St. Ernesto, who takes care of Pop every day;

To my love tsunami in motion, the community of friends and family that sustain me, a love tsunami I did not know the extent of until breast cancer. I consider that one of the greatest gifts, to learn that you are truly loved far and wide and that people will do their best when given a chance;

To Swarthmore Friends Meeting folks who did serious prayers, food, and accompaniment;

To Amy, taking me to doctors' appointments and stayed the night with me after surgery and being the BEST PA sis; Sue, who accompanied me in surgery and chemo; Alice, who sang to me over the phone while I waited for surgery; Sharon, who took me to doctors' appointments and most of my chemo sessions (made me the finest picnic lunches and helped me move with an IV in my arm) and cut my hair; Elizabeth, who prayed as Sharon cut my hair and invited Jesus to join us in chemo; Sally, who kept a change of clothes in her car in case I needed someone to stay with me;

So many prayers and sweet emails and cards that I have not always been able to keep up;

Women's Voices who named what I have done as Living Out Loud;

All who came to celebrate life and aliveness for my birthday when treatments were done;

All the people I have not seen in years who showed up since I had cancer;

The 900 million pray-ers;

All those who do art with me;

All those with whom I can share the depths of my spiritual life;

Friends and friends!! Pendle Hill, especially John! EEers, especially my support groups! Oak Womyn Drummers, especially Brenda! Potluckers! 2nd Friday Sharers (especially Joan, Joanne, Zu, Karen & Hank)! Clearness Committees! Cloggers (Meg, Mimi)! Fellow writers everywhere! Cultural Creatives! EIers;

PA Breast Cancer Coalition and especially Dolores, who reassured me early on;

Sue Weldon and UNITE FOR HER: who gave me the most special gifts of: half a share of CSA and opportunities for acupuncture, yoga, massage, nutrition analysis;

Chris: food, listener for writing project, sewed my pants, clerked my clearness committee, came to my arts and spirituality reception, constant affirmation, fruit cake I liked, and so much more;

Audrey: knitted a scarf, Trader Joe gift certificate, frequent check-ins, comes to Swarthmore meeting for her birthday (and the meeting sang to her and Shelley made her a cake – so sweet), sang me lullabies on the phone, and hosted a celebration;

Amy - facilitated contributions – oh my!!, almost daily check-ins, gives me needed frequent advice cuz she did this two years ago, shared her doctors with me, and so much more;

Dot - faithful Sunday friend, weekly beautiful pictures and Sunday emails;

I love Dot's new dog, Winston; he smiles with his teeth bared – never seen that before. Made me smile with my teeth bared;

Alice - supporter at work, hat with creatures, jacket, food, and checks on me often, made me healthy breast beads to make necklaces out of (a lot of people have already gotten a good laugh about these) and so much more;

Zu – who sings to me - whose heart now longs for Viet Nam; may her heart have its deepest longings and find its home;

Joan who takes me to the airport and is just always there;

Shelley - Reiki close and distant;

Zan – the best ever person to facilitate a class with;

PH students – the best ever class to do art with – nourished my heart and soul bigly and let me know that theirs were nourished as well! Lots of folks came to our Art receptions – the best;

Sally P - my Arts and Spirituality mentor: wishing me "lotsa hoopla as you swirl your way into radiant health" and so much encouragement in so many arenas. She taught me to turn to my creativity to get through the hard stuff;

Barbarejene W - the best spiritual nurturer ever, even by email;

Wayne (my downstairs housemate) – checks on me morning and night and provides me great music to listen to – I love it! Alex, Frank, Steve, Ellen & Jado for all that music;

Tom for Peace and Theresa – for all those years of friendship and peace music;

Tim - my second longest friend of 44 years now - flowers, songs and conversation - a very special concert;

Pat R and Laura R - KY companions who have been my friends for a long time and inspire me;

Huberta - my friend since we were 2;

Nancy S - emails, food, frequent check-ins, and took me to my first 3-D movie;

Mariellen - record numbers of emails and reading my writings;

Marcelle - one of the best pray-ers in the world;

Paul for Peace - my spiritual friend: conversations, clearness and worship;

Paul I - helps me out when I need help;

Betty B - my Lexington Friend who sends cards and inspirations and encourages me to write;

Joanna J - the healer and intuitive;

Marianne - house dusting;

Winnie - house cleaning twice - thanks to Reason for Cleaning for the volunteer program;

Ruth & Alice - faithful workplace colleagues who bring pumpkin soup and good cheer;

Catherine and Kathy - food and flowers;

Marie - filthyfarmgirl.com chapstick;

Brian, who has a poem for every occasion;

Cousin Madeline thought of my bald head while in Nepal and bought me a gorgeous scarf - my bald head is so grateful for all those beautiful scarves and hats to keep it warm and stylish;

Lynn M, Marge, and Gloria - made me beautiful scarves;

The blind lady in Media - made me two hats;

Ruth, Kim P, Pat, Bruce and Sharman – lovely work supporters – notes, hat, creams, offers of numerous ways of helping; Kim Mc, who says I get her to think about really hard stuff; Jeanette, who says I inspire her; Melissa, a bracelet for healing;

Cards and prayers galore from Lexington Friends Meeting;

Prayer shawls from Media Meeting's Prayer Shawl Ministry and from Whittier Knittiers;

Aunt Bet – for the gift of sabbatical with less stress because she remembered my mom in her will. Thank you, Aunt Bet! – thank you, other aunts and uncles – Pat, Nancy & Vern, Jane & Bobby for being out there and remembering my birthday;

Dee and James and Joe and Megan – took care of me and Pop when we went to Oregon;

Niece Janet for hand-made paper from Korea and the best monster ever;

Robyn – prayers sent on her blog, beautiful hand-made cards, and art supplies;

Meredith – who gives me hope in my work place;

Morgan – for the hoopin';

Helene, Hoot, and all the Friends of Jesus who enjoy my light-hearted Jesus stories;

Zakiya - who prays for me and cooks wonderful food;

My next door neighbors Pat and Lee - mowed some of my grass and love all the music (thankful for that);

My neighbor Kate - checks in and made me food;

Chuck – who recently appeared after not seeing him for a few years to remind me of the importance of doing work of substance;

Lynne H – who takes me to appreciate art at the Barnes;

Rich and Claudia – keep that singin' happenin';

Dr. Steve Bagnato – who helps me remember my profession as I have loved it;

All of my many doctors, especially Dr. Weiss, Dr. Gavis, Dr. Fried, Dr. Gilman, Dr. Fagan and Dr. Rooklin;

Bj, Jan and the folks at Rhythms for …poems, quotes, and stories;

Special thank yous to Melanie, Brenda, Barbarajene, and Jan for permission to include your poems and stories.

Finding My Way Through

Resource Notes

I highly recommend: The Clearness Committee - A Communal Approach To Discernment by Parker J. Palmer. This is a process used by Quakers for discernment that is wonderful!

www.couragerenewal.org/clearnesscommittee

UNITE for HER gave me the best gifts ever such as fresh organic vegetables from a Community Supported Agriculture coop in Lancaster. For fund raising, I highly recommend them. **www.uniteforher.org**

Dr. Weiss recommends: **www.breastcancer.org**

PA Breast Cancer Coalition: **www.pabreastcancer.org**

Cleaning For A Reason: **www.cleaningforareason.org**

Please join me on my website and blogsite: **www.jenelam.com**

Other books by this author:

Dancing with God Through the Storm: Mysticism and Mental Illness

Are You There God, Or Am I Going Crazy

My Angel Came

Humanity Emerging

JENNIFER ELAM is a licensed psychologist who studied, researched, taught and practiced psychology from 1969 until 2014. For most of her career, she taught at the college level, worked in residential treatment and worked in schools with students aged preschool through adulthood.

In 2012, she went on an adventure with breast cancer and worked through chemo and radiation. This book is about her spiritual journey through cancer. In 2014, Jennifer was diagnosed with pudendal neuralgia and had to retire (at least for now, she says).

Presently, Jennifer leads art retreats, is active in her Quaker community, helps to care for her elderly parents, and makes time to write, paint, pray, and enjoy ordinary life.

www.ingramcontent.com/pod-product-compliance
Lightning Source LLC
Chambersburg PA
CBHW050601300426
44112CB00013B/2017